The 16% Solution

How to Get High Interest Rates in a Low Interest World with Tax Lien Certificates

Joel S. Moskowitz, J.D.

Andrews and McMeel
A Universal Press Syndicate Company
Kansas City

Designed by Barrie Maguire.

Library of Congress Cataloging-in-Publication Data

Moskowitz, Joel S.
    The 16% solution : how to get high interest rates in a low
interest world with tax lien certificates / Joel S. Moskowitz.
        p. cm.
    Includes bibliographical references.
    ISBN 0-8362-8084-9
    1. Real estate investment. 2. Tax liens. I. Title. II. Title:
The sixteen percent solution.
HD1382.5.M69 1994
332.63'24—dc20   94-38967
                                                                CIP

Attention: Schools and Businesses

Andrews and McMeel books are available at quantity discounts with bulk purchase for educational, business, or sales promotional use. For information, please write to: Special Sales Department, Andrews and McMeel, 4900 Main Street, Kansas City, Missouri 64112.

Contents

Preface

Like millions of others, you are probably wondering where to put your money in these low interest times. Money market funds, banks, and savings and loans are paying less than 5% interest. After taxes and inflation, a 5% return leaves you with nothing at all.

Eager for higher yields, you may be considering joining millions of others who are rushing into an already overpriced stock market. Or you may be considering buying bonds, options, or more exotic instruments that may one day cost you some or most of your principal.

There is an alternative. An investment that will allow you to reap ultra-high yields. An investment that will allow you to sleep at night. An investment you can get into with very little money. An investment that is fun. I wrote this book to introduce you to that investment, known as tax lien certificates.

Tax lien certificates are not some new invention of a brokerage. They are issued by over 1,200 local governments in a majority of states. Banks, savings and loans, and many knowledgeable investors hold them. Now it's your turn to find out about them, your turn to profit from them.

Frankly, I'm excited for you. You are in for a wonderful, profitable discovery, and I am delighted to be your guide and companion.

Los Angeles, California

Joel S. Moskowitz

SECTION 1
Why You Need Tax Lien Certificates

CHAPTER 1
What Are Tax Lien Certificates?

A Tale of Two Brothers

Andy's heart sank. When he retired five years ago, his retirement nest egg of $100,000 was earning him 8% in the money market. That extra $667 each month, supplementing his Social Security, went a long way toward making his retirement comfortable. But these last years, he had been watching his interest rates steadily drop, until this last month he earned just $280 in interest.

Andy had so many plans. A trip with Carol to visit the kids in California. Adding on a guest room for visits from the grandchildren. Buying that small boat to go fishing on the lake. Now he and his wife would have to dip deeper into their principal each month, just to keep up their present lifestyle. And that would hurt their future income. He could see in the distance a time when their money was gone before they were.

Andy's brother Jay, on the other hand, put his money into Arizona tax lien certificates. Although they had saved a similar amount from their jobs, Jay's nest egg had been growing and compounding at a steady 16% for many years. At retirement, Jay had $325,000, all of which was still making 16% despite what was happening to interest rates in the rest of the economy! Jay was raking in an additional $50,000 a year! With that money, he and his wife were traveling, and had just bought a condo in Palm Beach.

Today, you will have to search for a certificate of deposit paying more than 6%. While some experts believe that rates will rise somewhat in future years, others observe that today's rates are more in line with those that have existed during most of this century.

This presents you with a major problem, particularly if you live or intend to live on the income produced by your savings.

Today, you will have to search for a certificate of deposit paying more than 6%.

If you are like most people, you are struggling, without much success, to get the yield back into your savings. The places to which you are turning are not producing much relief.

As of this writing, the following are typical yields on common investments:

5-year Treasury Note	6.2%
10-year Treasury Bonds	6.14%
15-year Mortgage-Backed Securities	7.5%
High Grade Corporate Bonds	7.06%
Money Market Funds	3.2%
Utility Stocks	6.3%
1-year Certificates of Deposit	4.2%

Several of these investments present peculiar risks. In chapter 3, we will consider in detail how to compare investments and combine them into a complete strategy. For the moment, we need to reflect that, particularly after taxes and inflation, these yields are very low.

A Tale of Two Cities

Bridgeport, Connecticut: *Bridgeport was in trouble. Maybe not as much trouble as it had been when the state was forced to step in and guarantee a $35 million deficit bond. Still, the bond money was gone, and this year the city faced a $20 million deficit in its $320 million budget.*

Bridgeport had just elected Joseph Ganim to be its mayor. Looking over the city's financial statement, he noticed that $9.25 million in property taxes were owed, a number that was growing during the recession. He and the city's finance director, Richard Robinson, went before the state's Review Board to proposef that Bridgeport be the first city in Connecticut to sell tax lien certificates. Mr. Robinson explained that if the liens were sold "we're going to see a number of individuals who have used the city as their bank say, 'Wait a minute, they're getting serious.'"[1]

New York City: *By the end of its 1991 fiscal year, New York City was owed over $500 million in property taxes. A* *group of real estate professionals, naming themselves "Collect," complained that the failure of some people to pay their taxes meant that taxes would have to be raised on the rest of the community to make up the shortfall. It proposed that the sale of tax lien certificates would allow a property tax cut. This, in turn, would encourage businesses to stay in the city. Further, said Collect, getting those dollars into the city's pocket would help pay for vital city services.*

The property owners, they noted, would owe exactly the same penalty anyway. What difference did it make if they owed it to the city or to an investor?

Not everyone was pleased with the idea. Some officials thought that the city should continue to earn the 18% penalty, rather than pay it to investors. Others replied that the city was very slow to collect, if it collected at all. One attorney was concerned for his clients, because a private investor would obtain the delinquent property more promptly than the city, which he could "jerk around for three or four years."[2]

One side effect of the recent recession is that many property owners cannot or will not pay their taxes. Local governments, which depend on those taxes to provide services, find it difficult to budget, or even to function, if the taxes owed do not arrive on time.

They can, and do, assess high penalties for failure to pay, and they have the power to foreclose upon the property. The problem with these solutions is that while they are being pursued, the government is without its money.

Certainly, the local government would, in ideal circumstances, rather collect and keep the penalty itself. However, it is in the same situation as the delinquent taxpayers, who, in ideal times, would rather pay the tax and be spared the penalty. Local governments are not in the lending business and, strapped for cash to provide immediate essential services, they do not have money to loan.

Local governments, which depend on those taxes to provide services, find it difficult to budget, or even to function, if the taxes owed do not arrive on time.

Certainly, the local government would, in ideal circumstances, rather collect and keep the penalty itself. However, it is in the same situation as the delinquent tax-payers, who, in ideal times, would rather pay the tax and be spared the penalty.

By stepping into the shoes of the government, you have a right to get the government's interest, and have the same rights over the property that the government would have.

Tax Lien Certificates: A Solution for Two Problems

Bridgeport and New York City are deciding whether to do what over 500 local governments in 29 states are already doing—issuing tax lien certificates. These certificates solve the government's need for a predictable, adequate cash flow, while solving the investor's need for a safe, high rate of interest. The government does not mind your getting the high rate of interest, because the government is not paying it. The property owners in the community who are paying taxes are thankful that their taxes do not need to be raised to make up the shortfall. Even the property owners who are delinquent do not care if you get this interest because the same penalty would have to be paid whether the government had sold the certificate or not. This is simply one of those rare situations where there are no losers, and big winners.

Tax lien certificates work like this:

Unpaid taxes become a lien on the property. This means that the tax obligation is recorded in the government's property records, and until the taxes are paid, the lien remains. If the taxes are not paid for a long enough period, the owner will lose the property. Meanwhile, a penalty of from 8% to 50% per year is being added to the amount of the lien. Having a lien on the property means that nobody can buy the property without being subject to the lien. Government-issued tax liens are super-safe, being superior even to first mortgages.

To get their money quickly, many local governments sell their liens to private investors, and issue certificates for the liens. Just as with the government, a penalty is added to the lien while the taxes remain unpaid. Similarly, just as with the government, the property will be forfeited to the investor if the lien is not paid off.

By stepping into the shoes of the government, you have a right to get the government's interest, and have the same rights over the property that the government would have.

"Tax Lien" States v.
"Tax Auction" States

The variety of state laws ensures that there is a state whose system fits your needs.

A comparison between California and Florida will help explain the difference between buying a tax lien and buying a property:

In California, if an owner does not pay the property taxes, the property becomes "tax defaulted" and the owner has five years to redeem the property. If the owner redeems, he must pay interest, penalties, and costs to the tax collector. If the owner does not redeem, the tax collector can sell the property.[3] *The buyer at this sale will never be paid any interest.* He is bidding on the property, and that is all he will get.

In Florida, by buying a tax lien certificate, you are purchasing the right to collect interest on the unpaid taxes. An auction is held, at which the successful bidder is the person who agrees to accept the lowest rate of interest from the property owner. However, all tax lien certificates not sold at the auction can be bought from the county, and will draw a full 18% interest without bidding. *In Florida, you are not buying the property; you are buying the right to interest on the unpaid taxes.* If the property owner still does not pay his taxes, then the property will be auctioned off. At this *second* sale, the bidders are after the property, not the interest.[4]

Each state can enact its own laws on subjects such as tax liens. As a result, there are many states where you can buy the right to interest on unpaid taxes, and yet if the taxes plus interest are still not paid, you can get the property without having to bid again—or pay any more money. Getting property this way does not happen often, but it happens often enough to keep the process interesting. The variety of state laws ensures that there is a state whose system fits your needs.

In this book, I will be focusing on states where your investment will bring you a high rate of interest, together with a high level of security. In these states, you *can* be delighted if the taxes are not paid, because you may then get the property for pennies on the dollar. I will tell you exactly how to do this.

First, however, I will explain in detail the mechanics of

how tax lien certificates work and how to buy them. The point I want to make here is that this is not an exotic, concocted investment, but a government-run program that serves the interests of the government as well as your interests. You can therefore rely upon its legitimacy, as you move on to learn its rules.

These ideas are likely new to you, so to get you primed for the adventure, in the next two chapters I will discuss what a world of difference the increased earnings of tax lien certificates will make to your investment program, and how an investment in tax lien certificates compares to your present investments.

Notes

1. Quoted in Hampton, "Bridgeport Board Proposed Selling Property Tax Liens to Raise Revenues." Vol. 299, *The Bond Buyer*, p. 373 (January 23, 1992).

2. Quoted in Weiss, "Group Suggests NYC Sell Tax Liens." Vol. 38, *Real Estate Weekly*, p. 1A (December 11, 1991).

3. Cal. Rev. & Tax Code 126, 3691–92, 3707, 3426, 4101–2.

4. A complete explanation of Florida's procedures is found in appendix 2.

CHAPTER 2
Why Would You Want a Tax Lien Certificate?

Tax lien certificates present you with an outstanding package of benefits:

High Yield

The main attraction of tax lien certificates is their consistently high yield.

Exactly how high this yield is depends upon where you invest. In Arizona, the top rate is 16%. Florida pays up to 18%. In Michigan, tax lien certificates yield up to 50% in the second year you hold them. When tax lien certificates are bought at auction, your actual rate is determined by competitive bid. If this sounds confusing (and it should), I will explain the procedures of the various states in later chapters. If you cannot stand to wait, you can consult the comparative chart in appendix 1.

The point here is that tax lien certificates should be prized as a high- yield interest investment. At these rates of interest, this is more than just nice—it is a road to real wealth.

To get an idea of what a real difference those extra percentage points make, use the "Rule of 72." This is a quick way of telling how long it will take you to double your money. It works like this: Whatever your percentage of interest, divide it into 72. The answer will tell you how many years it will take your principal to double.

For example, if you are earning 5% at a bank, your money will double in somewhat over 18 years. A corporate bond yielding 8% will double your money in nine years. An 11% return in the stock market (the historical average) will double your money in just over six and a half years. By contrast, keeping your money in Florida tax liens at 18% will double your money in four years!

How important is the difference? Let's take a hypothetical investor who places $2,000 in a retirement plan at age 25. And let's be fair and assume that her investment averages 8% a year for each of the next 40 years. By the time she is 65, at this 8% rate her money would have doubled over four times. By contrast, had she invested in tax lien certificates earning 18%, her money would have doubled about 10 times. And how much would she have made? Believe it or not, at 8% our investor would now have around $43,000. At 18%, she would now have over $1,500,000. All from that one-time investment! Figure it out for yourself—our investor would retire as a millionaire from that one investment in high-yielding tax lien certificates!

Safety

The second important trait of tax lien certificates is their safety. The tax lien certificates are *secured* by real property which has been appraised by a government agency at an amount usually 10 to 100 times the amount of the lien.

Certainly, high interest rates are available in certain risky investments, such as junk bonds, but if those do not pay off, there is no security for the money to which you can turn.

The Ability to Start Small

The saying "It takes money to make money" is certainly true. It does not need to be true, however, that it takes a lot of money to get a great return.

In tax lien certificates . . . you can get the same high return regardless of the size of your investment.

The saying "It takes money to make money" is certainly true. It does not need to be true, however, that it takes a lot of money to get a great return.

If you were buying a certificate of deposit, you might get a little more interest if you made a "jumbo" deposit of $50,000 or more. In tax lien certificates, by contrast, you can get the same high return regardless of the size of your investment. And because unpaid tax bills come in all sizes and you can buy just what you need, there will be an investment to suit your budget.

Unexpected Joy

While I emphasize the high interest rates provided by tax lien certificates, the possibility of obtaining property at un-heard-of bargain prices always exists, and many investors pursue tax lien certificates for just that purpose.

As I discuss in detail later, when you buy a tax lien in, for example, Arizona, if you are not paid back your principal plus interest, three years later you can obtain the property, free of any mortgage. That's right! I am not talking about bidding for the property at a tax sale. There will be no other bidders. You will get a Treasurer's Deed from the County Treasurer for just the cost of your tax liens!

This does not happen every day. But it does happen. And the thought that it could happen to you helps keep life interesting.

Tax-Deductible Travel

There is no rule that auctions of tax lien certificates need to be held at dull locations.

One of the most popular auctions of tax lien certificates is in Sedona, Arizona, in February. Sedona is a place where tourists flock all year to hike, go shopping for crafts, or visit the mysterious Seven Vortices. The mention of Palm Beach, Florida, conjures up such vivid images of palm trees and water that nothing more need be said.

If you are going to these locations for investment purposes, the cost of your travel is added for tax purposes to the cost of the certificates you buy and you will therefore pay less in taxes when you sell the certificates because you will have less of a profit. Further, if you can make the case that you are in the "business" of buying tax lien certificates, your travel expenses are deductible immediately. As a rule, you cannot deduct travel to learn about or investigate investment opportunities.

There is no rule that auctions of tax lien certificates need to be held at dull locations.

"Bragging Rights"

Certainly, there are few topics more talked about than investments. Fred will talk about a hot stock which he bought on a hot tip just before it soared.

But Fred won't tell you about his investments that failed. And he won't make you confident that he can repeat his coup very often.

When you invest in tax lien certificates you will have guaranteed yourself bragging rights. And your story need not be limited to the success you had last month, but can include your system, which will reliably make you a winner next month—and every month. Your friends will know that this was not luck—they will think you are one smart person. And you are.

CHAPTER 3
How Do Tax Lien Certificates Fit Into Your Investment Plans?

Asked how he liked being 80 years old, Maurice Chevalier replied, "Considering the alternative, I like it fine." When it comes to investments, the only real answer to why you should put your money in tax lien certificates is that they are the best alternative for your investment plans.

Tax lien certificates are the best vehicle for your investment plans.

That statement is especially meaningful, because if there is one thing this world does not lack, it is investment choices: Real Estate Investment Trusts, January Pork Belly Futures, Oil Drilling Limited Partnerships, Collateralized Mortgage Obligations, Callable Convertible Zero Coupon Debentures. We wander through a marketplace filled with sales agents grasping for any spare buck that manages to escape the tax man and the grocer.

One thing they all say is that you are a fool to put your money in anything as absurdly old-fashioned as a bank.

> Fred, at 5% interest you are losing money after taxes and inflation. But for the last eight years, Hogshead contracts have gone up at least 15 cents each May. Even if the price goes up only 10 cents this year, your $10,000 investment will grow to $17,000!

True enough, and if the price goes down only 10 cents, your hard-earned investment will shrink to $3,000!

If you had the mind of a medieval monk and the patience of a boulder, you could pore over endless charts and financial statements. But even though modern life is filled with competing demands, the usual methods of choosing investments—from guesswork, tips, and hope—will not do. If your choices are to reliably stand the test of time, you will have some serious comparison shopping ahead of you. To talk meaningfully about the proper place of tax lien certificates, then, we need to talk about the rest of the world. In this chapter, you will be

Just as everything written in the English language is composed of just 26 letters and just as every color imaginable is composed of a mixture of only three primary colors, so every possible investment product is composed of a mixture of a few primary traits.

pulled away from the noise and confusion of individual investment products so that you can take a moment and review and compare factors common to all investments.

Just as everything written in the English language is composed of just 26 letters and just as every color imaginable is composed of a mixture of only three primary colors, so every possible investment product is composed of a mixture of a few primary traits.

To the sophisticated investor to whom this discussion will sound like old hat, remember that every great athlete spends the most time practicing fundamentals, not fancy strokes. You may be in more need of this break than a novice. Let us make a small side bet that after you read this chapter, you will find yourself thinking of your old investments in a new light.

Risk-Reward: Trite and True

A college professor tells the story of a final examination he once supervised. While all of the other students were hurriedly completing their tests, one student had not even begun to write. When asked what the problem was, the student said:

> "In preparing for this exam, I condensed the entire semester's work onto one page. I then condensed that page into one paragraph. Next, I condensed that paragraph into one sentence. Finally, I condensed that sentence into one word. But I forgot the word."

"That's baloney," the professor replied, disgusted. "That's the word!" rejoiced the student.

Just as the student in the above story managed to abstract a subject until the result was meaningless, so the principle of risk-reward is too abstract a tool to result in a concrete plan of action. There is a fundamental wisdom in the principle of finding the right balance between risk and reward, but like most fundamental truths, it is so pervasive and condensed as to be overlooked, or dismissed as commonplace.

Every abstraction works only by dropping off unique characteristics of the subject being abstracted. In investing, those unique characteristics will distinguish success from failure.

For our purposes, then, we are going to expand the number of categories under both risk and reward to include those which will be truly helpful in analyzing tax liens and other investments.

Many investments are like money in a mattress, although this is not immediately obvious.

Reward Factors

Obviously, the essence of investing is the thought that placing what you currently have in a certain situation will result in your having more later. For the purpose of comparing investments, you should consider exactly by what mechanism your profit is expected to be produced. In general, this will be through (1) income potential or (2) growth potential.

Income Potential

The ability of an investment to earn you payments of money is its *income potential.* For example, if you put money in a bank, it will produce income in the form of interest. The money you put in the bank does not become more valuable (indeed, because of the effects of inflation, it becomes less valuable). But it earns *more* money, and so has income potential.

. . . all other factors being equal, an investment with income potential is better than one without it.

Not too long ago, many people put their savings in a mattress, or in a box buried under a tree. Leaving aside all other problems with these solutions, they clearly provided no income potential. If all went well, the money they took out would be the same money they put in; no more, no less.

Many investments are like money in a mattress, although this is not immediately obvious. If you buy a house to live in, while you hope that it will go up in value (a dim prospect in many areas at this time), unless you rent it out, it has no income potential.

Similarly, gold bullion or diamonds are often bought as a hedge against inflation or social disruption. They may or may not serve these purposes, and they may or may not increase in value, but they have no income potential.

Take it as a rule that, all other factors being equal, an investment with income potential is better than one without it.

The key phrase here is "all other factors being equal."

They never are. A failing corporation may be paying dividends through selling off its assets, which in turn may diminish its prospects for future profits. No mechanical rule is a substitute for thought.

Just because an investment has income potential does not mean that its payments are regular, or that you will be able to draw them out and live on them. It just means that the purpose of the investment is the production of payments.

Turning to tax liens, their obvious and superb strong point is their *income potential.* In fact, I know of no other safe investment which pays such consistently high rates of interest.

Growth Potential

Growth invest-ments require that you predict the future; income investments just ask you to wait for it.

The possibility that an item will increase in value is its *growth potential.* The hope here is that the item will decrease in supply or increase in demand so that its market value will go up. Every investment requires time. Income investments just ask you to wait for the future; growth investments require that you *predict* it.

Predicting the future is a risky business. Most people simply assume that whatever the trend is will continue. When a stock is rising, they assume that it will rise forever; when it is falling, they assume there is no floor. This is why most people sell investments when they are low and buy when they are high, which of course is exactly the opposite of what they should be doing.

As a general rule, competitive fortune-telling is a risky and unreliable way to make money.

One difficulty in foretelling the future is that it is influenced by more factors than can reasonably be considered. For example, real estate investors in Southern California and New England took seriously Will Rogers's thought that real estate would continue to make money because no one was making any more of it. That takes care of the issue of supply. But when economic conditions which were not widely predicted caused those areas to be less desirable as places to locate, and when prices had risen so high that it was impossible to qualify and pay for a loan, the absence of demand caused prices to suffer greatly.

The second problem with making money by fortune-telling is that it is a competitive game. By the time you read a brilliant analysis of the future of a stock in a financial magazine, other investors who read it first, or who just had the same ideas, may have bid up the price of the stock, discounting in advance the predicted events.

As a general rule, competitive fortune-telling is a risky and unreliable way to make money.

Tax lien certificates are not primarily growth investments. Their main attraction is their spectacularly high interest rate. Still, they are secured investments, and if the liens are not paid off, the property will be forfeited. This has occasionally resulted in spectacular growth opportunities for the holders of these certificates. Because their main purpose is income, however, tax lien certificates will perform very nicely whether they produce a property windfall or not. This feature sets them apart and above most growth investments.

Risk Factors

Market Risk

Market risk is the possibility that when you try to sell your investment, the marketplace will value it less than you did when you bought it.

The most obvious example is buying a stock at its high point, and later taking a loss when you sell after its value declines. All growth investments are subject to market risk, even those touted as immune.

For example, like most residents of Southern California, I was told that buying a home would be my best investment. It was pointed out that people in that area with the most modest incomes were rich in equity, because bungalows they bought after World War II for $11,000 were being sold for $80,000. Everyone recommended that I borrow as much as I could get to buy the most expensive home possible. The idea was that values would rise faster than their interest payments, and I would pocket the difference. This is known as the principle of *leverage.*

For years this worked. I bought a house for $60,000 and

Leverage is a powerful principle, but it works in both directions. It is a gun that sometimes fires backward.

sold it twelve years later for $150,000. Then I bought a house for $360,000 (borrowing even more money) and sold it only two years later for $550,000. The pace of this game was obviously quickening. I stretched and bought a house for $740,000.

Everyone was playing this game at the same time. It worked great! Until one day it didn't. I am writing this two years after buying this last house. It is on the market for $250,000 less than I paid. In a month, no one has even come to look at it.

Leverage is a powerful principle, but it works in both directions. It is a gun that sometimes fires backward. Today, hundreds of thousands of homeowners must, like me, repay their original purchase prices on homes which have gone down in value. There is no faster way to lose money.

Market risk comes in several forms and may be caused by internal or external factors. Internal factors relate to how well the business is doing. If it is faltering, the business and any shares in the business may reflect this decline. As an example of an external factor, bonds may be bought for their income, but if they are sold before maturity, their value to other investors will depend upon the interest rates that are available elsewhere. If interest rates have risen, the rate which the bond will pay becomes less attractive, and so its value will be lowered to compensate.

This last example illustrates that market risk is most often a feature of growth investments, rather than of income investments. If the bond is held to maturity as an income investment, market risk would not affect its value. Of course, bonds are subject to other risks, as discussed later in this chapter.

Tax lien certificates, like other income investments, carry no market risk. Delinquent property owners are compelled by law to pay high rates of interest; they have no real choice in the matter except to lose their properties.

As is discussed later, tax lien certificates have only limited liquidity. They therefore have no exposure, as do bonds on the secondary market, to fluctuating interest rates.

Safety

The sales agents at Lincoln Savings had a powerful argument to customers cashing in their certificates of deposit: "What is the point in renewing your CD when you can get twice the interest in our bonds?" The only problem was that a bond is just a promise to pay, and this promise was not kept.

Obviously, the CDs that Lincoln's customers cashed were safer than the bonds, because they were guaranteed by a federal insurance agency. But that agency itself has insufficient funds, and the only real safety lies in the hope that Congress will endlessly throw enough money to cover all its debts. Safety is a relative thing.

Concerning the safety of tax liens, the vast majority of tax liens are paid off with interest. For example, the *Orlando Sentinel* reported that less than 1% of tax liens remain unpaid within two years.[1] Still, we must remember that tax lien payers are a class of already delinquent people, whose credit ratings we know nothing about. If you were to look at a tax lien certificate as a promissory note, it would be a miserable investment.

But tax lien certificates are more: they are a *secured* investment. If the landowner does not pay off the lien, you, as the holder of the tax lien certificate, can look to the property itself to pay off the lien. Because the amount of the tax lien is rarely more than a small percent of the value of the property, this lien is completely secured.

By comparison, mortgage holders think that they are well secured if their loan is no more than 75% of the value of the property. They feel confident that the property will not drop by more than 25% of the appraised value until the loan is substantially paid down or paid off. Granted, the current savings and loan crisis was caused in part by those valuations underestimating the potential decline in land value in certain parts of the country, such as Texas. Still, a tax lien certificate rarely represents more than 5% of the property's value, and is senior even to the first mortgage holder. The chance of a decline of more than 95% in the property's value from the county's appraisal is remote. This is obviously why these liens are almost always paid off. They are so thoroughly secured that only a rare property owner would let the property be sold for this debt.

Liquidity

The liquidity of an investment refers to your ability to sell it relatively quickly; to convert it into cash.

The risk of loss of liquidity is twofold:

First, there is the possibility that you will require the money invested so quickly that you will suffer a significant loss. This loss can come in the form of the familiar "substantial penalty for early withdrawal" which is imposed when funds in a certificate of deposit are withdrawn before the certificate matures. It is also reflected in the "desperate owner" advertisements for home sales which are common today.

Second, in case the investment should start to slide in value, lack of liquidity will keep you on for a longer ride downward. Thus, when interest rates fell in recent years, those invested in money markets could shift their funds easily and without penalty. When home prices fell during the same period, sellers were unable to unload their houses quickly, if at all.

In the case of limited liquidity, higher reward tends to follow higher risk. Thus, financial institutions tend to pay higher interest rates on their longer-term certificates of deposit.

Liquidity is undeniably a weak point of tax lien certificates. While the certificate can in most cases be assigned, and while a small brokerage market, limited partnerships, and a mutual fund are emerging (see appendix 4), there is no established secondary market for them, as there is for stocks and bonds. Anyone investing in tax liens needs to assume the worst case—that the money will be unavailable until the debtor pays or the property can be sold.

Indeed, tax lien certificates display a form of unpredictable liquidity, as the property owner can pay off the lien at any time. This feature is worse than callable bonds, where the issuer is at least limited to certain time periods for redemptions. Still, bondholders typically redeem early because prevailing interest rates have gone down. The rate of return on tax lien certificates is set by law; so long as suitable certificates are available, the money can be quickly turned over to new certificates paying the same high rate.

Overhead

Overhead is the expense of your operation. You cannot directly get it back, regardless of the success of the venture. For example, if a sales agent goes to visit a prospect, the cost of the gasoline he burns to get there is overhead. The sales agent hopes that the profit from the sale will justify the expense, but those funds are gone in any case.

In a sense one cannot talk about overhead as a "risk," as those funds have been lost. Still, it is useful to think of overhead in this way, because the risk refers to the possibility that the eventual reward will not justify the cost to you.

Overhead need not necessarily be directly financial. Your labor has a market value, and if you spend your time canvassing a neighborhood as a door-to-door salesman, talking to brokers, or even researching investments, the time you spend is overhead.

The reason this risk is mentioned here is to distinguish those investments that require personal time, effort, and money from those that don't.

Because there presently is only a small secondary market for tax lien certificates, locating and purchasing them requires a certain investment of time and money. At the far end of the scale, this may involve the time and costs of travel to the location of an auction. At the other end of the scale, it may involve no more than the cost of a call to local officials to verify the existence of "leftover" certificates and the nature of the property.

Still, this amounts to more time and effort than that involved in calling a broker and ordering a stock or a bond. In those cases, the cash overhead is limited to the broker's commissions, and the time overhead is limited to whatever research went into the selection.

The overhead in tax lien certificates may be deductible; the time investment in traveling, perhaps to resorts such as Telluride, Colorado, and Miami, Florida, may be enjoyable, but in the current state of the market, tax lien certificates are a hand-picked investment.

Dealing With Risk

The level of comfortable risk is determined in large part by personality. Appropriate risk, however, depends as much or more on external factors.

There are several ways that you can respond to risk:

Risk Avoidance

The most primitive response to risk is complete avoidance. Because risk is a negative thing, this might at first seem to be the most sensible response. And it might sometimes be, if it were possible. For example, you might conclude that because all investments have risks, you should convert your savings into paper money and place the cash in a safe deposit box. You would then have successfully avoided investment risk. (Further, this would be a great tax strategy, for without gain, there is no tax.) On the other hand, not only is this money earning nothing, but its value is being steadily eroded by inflation, and so in place of risk you get a certainty of loss. Low-earning, extremely conservative investments, such as insured bank certificates of deposit, most often ensure a loss, as the rate of inflation plus the income taxes you must pay exceed your rate of return.

Risk Management

The middle approach to risk is *management*. This involves determining and controlling the level of risk you are prepared to take, and then locating those investments which will produce the greatest return for that level of risk.

Your level of comfortable risk is determined in large part by your personality. Appropriate risk, however, depends as much or more on external factors. For example, the level of risk which can be taken by a young person is greater than that of a retiree, because in a worst-case event, the young person may be able to earn the money back; the retiree cannot. Because the level of reward tends to follow the level of risk, young people are often counseled to follow their adventurous instincts in hope of larger gains. Other factors, such as job and marital status and amount of savings must likewise influence sensible exposures to risk. For example, a young person with only a few dollars in savings is unwise to invest those scarce dollars in aggressive growth stocks, even if the risk is otherwise appropriate to his age.

While you certainly need to figure out your level of comfortable risk and the chances of your investment getting you into trouble, you cannot just calculate the odds and see what happens; you need to reduce the likelihood of your nightmare coming true; you need to employ risk management techniques.

The first technique of risk management is diversification. If you have studied computer stocks and believe that IBM, Apple, and Compaq all have identical upside potential and identical risks, you should invest in *all* of them if your aim is to avoid large downside exposure. Even better diversity would be achieved by placing some of your funds outside of the computer field altogether. Of course, logic will tell you that unless the risks are linked (such as insuring three packages on one ship against a disaster at sea) you are actually more likely to suffer some loss through diversification. Still, you are less likely to suffer a major loss.

Diversification need not be simply between products. One can diversify through time as well. Rather than fully investing all at once, if investments are spread over time, the chances of having invested at a high point in the market and therefore suffering exposure to a down market are reduced. Of course, the chances of benefiting from having fully invested at the market's low point are lessened as well. As in the case of diversification between products, the theory of spreading investments over time is that the market as a whole will do well enough and no one is wise or lucky enough to consistently time strategic moves.

The greatest protection against risk, however, does not lie in the mechanical tricks of product diversification or dollar cost averaging, but rather in sticking to quality. In any market, certain investments protect their owners better than others. Finding candidate investments, researching them before making a commitment, and knowing when to get rid of them, all re-

The greatest protection against risk . . . does not lie in the mechanical tricks of product diversification or dollar cost averaging, but rather in sticking to quality.

quire attention, courage, and often dull homework. Knowing the risks to which each investment is subject is the first step.

Risk Exploitation

The highest level of response to risk is exploitation. One of my clients, for example, buys old oil fields and cleans them up for residential development. The marketplace hates old oil fields, as they may be pockmarked with imperfectly abandoned wells and oily deposits, and their risks are not widely understood. However, with expert investigation of the property, my client can take advantage of the market's aversion to the risks presented by these properties and buy them at a discount far deeper than would be required by the cost of cleanup.

Risk exploitation is most successful when a single investor's close-up experience identifies situations that the market overlooked, or reveals inaccuracies in the market's perceptions. Because the marketplace is always on the lookout for opportunity, risk exploitation is often a creature of luck.

Putting It Together: The Place of Tax Lien Certificates in Your Investment Strategy

The typical investment advice you will hear is to divide your cash between money market funds, stocks, and bonds. The theory is that the money market funds provide liquidity, the bonds provide steady income and a hedge against interest rates falling, and the stocks provide an opportunity for growth. Through your life cycle, the proportion on these investments is supposed to change, with growth stocks being less represented as one ages.

In the current market, this strategy makes no sense. The stock market as of this writing is at historic highs both in absolute terms and as measured against the earnings of the underlying companies. It is, by most calculations, overbid, and is sustaining its record prices through an astonishing application of the "greater fool theory." With interest rates the lowest that have been seen in years, bonds are in great danger, as their value will fall as interest rates rise, and interest rates have nowhere else to go.

Tax lien certificates, on the other hand, are greatly out-performing the bond market, and are doing far better than the long-term performance of the stock market, without its vola-tility. In this market, tax lien certificates can easily occupy the place in your portfolio that stocks, or bonds, or both, are usu-ally recommended to fill. All that is lost in this transition is the liquidity of stocks and bonds. But stocks and bonds are not recommended for their liquidity. Rather, money market funds are typically used for their liquidity. Indeed, stocks and bonds have always been recommended as investments to be held at least as long as is typical for tax lien certificates.

. . . tax lien certif-icates can easily occupy the place in your portfolio that stocks, or bonds, or both, are usually rec-ommended to fill.

As with any other investment, whether and how much li-quidity you need depends upon your financial and life situa-tion. Clearly, unless you are looking at assignable certificates and have a person ready, willing, and able to purchase them from you, placing all your spare cash in tax lien certificates would be a mistake.

On the other hand, with the interest rates on tax lien cer-tificates as high as they are, and with historic returns on stocks being only 11% or so, tax lien certificates can easily oc-cupy the place in your portfolio that growth investments, such as stocks, are usually recommended to fill.

As interest rates are hitting historic lows in the early 1990s, many people on fixed incomes are taking maturing certifi-cates of deposit and putting these funds into the stock market. This is almost certainly a mistake. Any investor who was in certificates of deposit in the first place was sufficiently so con-cerned about safety that turning to the stock market in search of higher yields can only be justified by ignoring the risk.

One characteristic common to many people on fixed in-comes is that they have time; they are most often retired. The time overhead of tax lien certificates therefore does not lie as heavy on these investors as on those who must personally pursue other sources of income. For these investors, care-fully-chosen tax lien certificates are ideal.

Without a doubt, investing is an art. You need to find the right balance of risk and reward which satisfies your needs for liquidity, safety, and growth. This is a constant challenge as the market changes, and as your needs change.

By working the unique and consistently profitable traits of tax lien certificates into your portfolio, you will have a top flight investment plan for the 1990s and beyond.

Notes

1. Snyder, "How to Make a Profit Paying Someone Else's Taxes." *Orlando Sentinel,* Business, p. 1 (April 19, 1990).

$ = Yes
Blank = No

Investment	Income Potential	Growth Potential	Avoids Market Risk	Safety	Liquidity
Tax Lien Certificates	$	$	$	$	
Residential Real Estate		inconsistent		$	
Rental Real Estate	inconsistent	inconsistent		$	
Stocks	inconsistent	inconsistent		inconsistent	$
High Grade Bonds	$	inconsistent		$	$
Certificates of Deposit	$		$	$	
Money Market Funds	$		$	$	$

Figure 1: Comparison of Sample Investments in the 1990s

SECTION 2
How You Can Buy Tax Lien Certificates

CHAPTER 4
Selecting an Area

CHAPTER 5
What to Look for in Properties

CHAPTER 6
Bidding at Local Auctions

CHAPTER 7
Armchair Values in "Leftovers"

CHAPTER 8
Buying from Other Investors

CHAPTER 9
Getting Local Officials to Help You

CHAPTER 4
Selecting an Area

The Chinese sage, Lao-tzu, observed: "A journey of a thousand miles must begin with a single step."[1] The dividing line between successful people and dreamers is the taking of that first step. In this case, your first step is to decide, out of all the country's possibilities, what one state and what one county will be the target of your first purchase of tax lien certificates.

Narrow the Available Range of States

Your first stop will be appendix 1 of this book, which lists the available states that sell tax lien certificates. Look them over now.

The states that are not on this list sell delinquent properties at auction. You may find good bargains in properties at these sales, just as you will at all foreclosure sales. That is not what we are discussing here, however. Here, we are aiming primarily for a secured investment with a high interest rate.

Consider Your Own State

Do you happen to live in one of the states listed in appendix 1? If you do, this will be a convenience to you, because you may be more familiar with the neighborhoods in the county you pick, and if you decide to travel to that area, either to attend a tax lien auction (see chapter 6, "Bidding at Local Auction") or to personally check out a property before you buy a lien from the tax collector (see chapter 7, "Armchair Values in 'Leftovers'") you will not have far to go. Further, as your collection of tax lien certificates grows, and as the time when you may be able to foreclose on one or more of these properties draws near, you may experience an intense curiosity to visit the neighborhood where you own tax liens.

For this reason, as you go through the additional considerations discussed below, if two states come close in your rankings, always give the nod to your home state

[I]f two states come close in your rankings, always give the nod to your home state.

The first factor you should look at if property is your goal is the general economic condition of the state.

As a second choice, give preference to a state in your region of the country. In my case, I live in California, a state which does not sell tax lien certificates. I am therefore partial to tax lien certificates issued by counties in Arizona.

Focus on Your Objective: Money or Property

Tax lien certificates are a unique investment in that they not only provide for a high rate of secured interest, they also provide the opportunity to obtain real estate at fabulously low prices. While I stress in this book the income potential of tax lien certificates, if you want to maximize the possibility of obtaining the property, you may be drawn to certain states.

The first factor you should look at if property is your goal is the general economic condition of the state. If a state is in a recession, with deeply depressed real estate prices and high unemployment, the chances that property will be forfeited are increased.

The second factor to consider is the laws of that state, and whether they assist the owner of a tax lien certificate in obtaining the property.

For example, while Florida allows a very nice 18% on tax lien certificates, it gives a tax lien buyer no special edge in obtaining the property. As you will see in appendix 2 ("The 16% Winner's Circle"), in Florida, if your tax lien certificate is not redeemed, you can apply for a tax deed. The deed will actually go to the person who bids the most for the property. You are allowed to bid in the amount you paid for your tax lien certificate, along with the interest you have earned. A complete stranger can show up, however, and bid a higher amount in cash and take the property. Clearly, Florida is a state you go to for the interest rate.

By contrast in Arizona, if the property owner does not redeem the tax lien certificate in three years, you can go to court and foreclose on the lien. After five years, you do not even need to go to court; you can just go in to the county treasurer and apply for a deed. There is no auction. You do not need to outbid anyone. You do not need to dig into your pocket for more money than you have already paid. In Colorado, you can likewise just bring your tax lien certificate to the county treasurer after three years and "the treasurer shall make out a deed." Arizona and Colorado are states that make it easy to get the property.

Maryland is an extreme example of a state *encouraging* the transfer of the property. There, you *must* foreclose within two years and, for certain properties, you may foreclose after only 60 days of obtaining your tax lien certificate!

Consider the Interest Rates

I have put interest rates last among factors to consider in selecting a state precisely because most people put it first. Obviously, if all other factors were equal, you are better off getting 24% interest than you are getting 18% interest. But all other factors are never equal.

For example, Michigan is well known as a state where you can get 50% interest on a tax lien in the second year. After you have obtained a tax deed, if the property owner wants to redeem, he must pay you 50% interest, regardless of when within that second year he redeems. The effective rate can be a hundred or more percent per year, if the redemption is early.

On the other hand, if you end up with no redemption, Michigan can be an awkward state, because at the auction in Michigan, you bid on what percentage of an "undivided interest" you will accept if there is no redemption. In other words, the property owner will be made your "involuntary partner."

You also need to consider that if a state has a high interest rate, that may mean that the competition is stiffer in that state. For example, in early 1992, Iowa doubled its interest rate to a whopping 24%. Before then, competition for Iowa tax lien certificates was pretty low. After that increase, however, county treasurers have had no trouble selling the liens. The plan of visiting rural counties to buy tax liens at full rates is a great one, but not if the deal is so overwhelming that others have beaten you there and there is little to choose from. You will always be better off with an actual 16% yield than a theoretical 24%.

Clearly then, you should avoid states with a low interest rate, but among states within a few points of each other, geography, economics, competition for the certificates, and other factors should be stressed.

Zero in on a County

There are over 1,200 counties to choose from in 29 states.

Although the rules for the sale of tax lien certificates are set by state law, the actual sales are made by local governments in each county. Even within a single state, the characteristics of counties will vary dramatically.

Your first decision in selecting a county is to decide whether you want an urban or a rural area. I personally favor rural counties, because the competition is often light and the staff has far more time and inclination to help me. Others prefer urban counties because there is a larger selection of properties or because they like the attractions of a particular city.

Again, you must ask whether you are looking for property or income. Counties vary in the percentage of properties that are redeemed.

Pinpoint a Neighborhood

Within every county, there is a "good" area, as well as an area "on the wrong side of the tracks." Certainly, you want your tax lien certificate to be on property in a desirable area.

There are several ways to check out areas within a county. A personal visit is a fine idea. Real estate brokers can help. One of the best sources, however, is the staff of the local tax collector. (See chapter 9, "Getting Local Officials to Help You.") These officials can tell you not only which areas are nicest, but also which areas produce the highest rates of redemptions.

Notes

1. Lao-tzu, *The Way of Life*, p. 64.

CHAPTER 5
What to Look for in Properties

Now that you have focused on a state, a county, and an area, your next step is to decide what kinds of properties you want to consider.

A great variety of properties are available. They range from undeveloped land to land developed for residential, commercial, or industrial uses.

At first glance, it might seem as though the kind of property you get is not an important question. All of these properties have been appraised as being worth much more than your tax lien certificate is going to cost. You might not mind getting any of these properties at such a low price.

However, what kind of property you get *can* make a big difference. One tax lien investor was quoted in *Forbes:* "I was buying everything I could get my hands on, but I didn't realize how much junk I bought."[1] Because he had to foreclose on several properties that were difficult to sell, he figures that he's lucky if he's broken even. He concludes: "It's like walking through a mine field. You get blown up eventually."[2] While the article rightly concludes that care is necessary for this investment, there is hardly any investment where you will be safe buying everything you can get your hands on.

Surely, you can take a wrong turn. For example, many parcels of raw land are sitting, alone, out in the middle of the desert, with no access to water or utilities and perhaps with no roads in the area. These parcels may often be zoned as residential, but this has no practical meaning. In chapter 13 ("'Worthless' Properties"), I go into more detail about the difficulties of an investment in raw land.

In an economic sense, the only value of land lies in what you can do with it. The best proof that land can be developed is that it has already been developed. No matter how high the appraisal on raw land may be, the pool of investors willing to check it out is small, and you could experience a long delay in selling it.

[T]he only value of land lies in what you can do with it. The best proof that land can be developed is that it has already been developed.

Industrial properties are susceptible to requiring expensive cleanups. (See chapter 14, "Environmental Problems.") Both industrial and commercial properties are valued for the revenue they can produce, and are therefore susceptible to economic downturns. Moreover, they tend to be expensive, and therefore reduce the diversification that is important to any investment.

As you can probably tell by now, I am steering you toward residential properties.

The reason for this is not that I am condemning investments in raw land or in commercial or industrial properties. To the contrary, vast fortunes have been made in such properties. My preference for residential properties lies rather in my focus on tax lien certificates as a secured, high interest rate investment. Residential properties provide the benefits without the occasional complications.

This view of tax lien certificates as an income investment requires that the properties be redeemed as high a percentage of the time as possible. Certainly, the motivation of a property owner to redeem his home exceeds his motivation to redeem any other investment.[3] Moreover, the problems, environmental and other, that might lead an owner to not want to redeem are far more rare in residential properties, as I discuss in detail in chapter 14.

However, all residential properties are not created equal. As I discuss in chapter 13, before you invest in a tax lien on a property, you need to have seen the assessment, and how it is broken down between the land and the improvements. As a rule of thumb, the improvements should represent 75% of the total assessment. If they fall below 60%, either there is a lot of acreage, the land is fabulous, or the improvements are below par. You should skip such an investment. Often, the "improvement" on a property, when it represents a smaller fraction of the value, is a mobile home or a shack.

In checking out a property, there is always a dilemma between wanting the benefits of the investigation and yet hating the costs. If you were buying a property, it might be worthwhile to spend $3,500 on an environmental investigation and $500 for a property inspection. One might also want to see who the lenders are and whether any of them have been taken over by the federal regulators. (See chapter 17, "FDIC/RTC Liens.") If all you are doing is investing $1,300 in a lien which has a 98% chance of being redeemed, it is impossible to justify much cost and effort.

Some properties are easy to check out. As one tax lien investor observed: "You can't go far wrong when it says yacht club."[4] One the other hand, he added, if you are careless, "You could end up with swamp land."[5]

In the end, the amount of effort and money you spend getting assurance that a property is a good place for your tax lien is a personal choice. My view, which I back up with my own money, is that the statistics of very high redemption rates, coupled with diversification, and buffered by extraordinarily high returns provides considerable comfort.

My advice to you is to augment that comfort by sticking to good neighborhoods, by investing only in improved properties, by limiting yourself to residential properties, and by checking the assessment to be sure that the improvement represents the lion's share of the value of the property.

At that point, if you cannot sleep easy, you probably weren't going to anyway.

[A]ugment [your] comfort by sticking to good neighborhoods, by investing only in improved properties, by limiting yourself to residential properties, and by checking the assessment to be sure that the improvement represents the lion's share of the value of the property.

Notes

1. Lubove, "Caveat Emptor." *Forbes*, p. 80 (December 24, 1990).

2. Ibid.

3. Smith, "Annual Tax Certificate Sale Under Way, Low-Risk Investing." *Palm Beach Post,* Financial Ed., Business, p. 5B (June 4, 1991).

4. Daniels, "Unpaid Tax Certificates Lure Investors." *Fort Lauderdale Sun-Sentinel,* Business, p. 1D (May 30, 1990).

5. Ibid.

CHAPTER 6
Bidding at Local Auctions

The centerpiece of excitement and social life among those who invest in tax lien certificates is the annual auction. Note that I didn't say that the auction is the best way to buy tax lien certificates. My recommendations for getting the best bargains are in chapter 7 ("Armchair Values in 'Leftovers'") and chapter 8 ("Buying From Other Investors"). Still, you have not fully experienced the world of tax lien certificates until you have gone to the auction.

When Is the Auction?

States that offer tax lien certificates generally hold an auction once each year. A few states allow counties to hold additional auctions of "leftovers," but these are rare. Exactly when the auction will be is outlined in state law, but can often vary a little by county.

For example, in Arizona each county holds its auction in February (which, incidentally, is a very nice month to visit Arizona). Colorado counties hold their auctions the second Monday in December (which, if you are a skier, is a very nice month to visit Colorado). In Florida, that auction is around June 1 (not a bad time to be in Florida). I am sure you are seeing a pattern here, and an extra reason to go to the auctions.

As soon as you have determined the state and the county you want to buy in, you should be contacting the local county tax collector, sometimes called the county treasurer, to find out the date, time, and place of the next auction.

What Properties Are Available?

While you are on the phone asking the treasurer about the auction, ask how you will be able to get a list of available properties. Each state's law requires the list of properties, along with at least some sort of description and the amount of taxes owed, to be published in the local newspaper. On the other hand, it is an awful bother to have to subscribe to the newspaper to get the list and you would then end up knowing far more than you ever cared about the local doings in Hugmarump County.

The list is most often posted in the office of the tax collector, but that too is probably not a convenient location for you. Some tax collectors will keep spare copies of the newspaper for sale in their offices, and will mail you a copy for 25¢ plus postage. Happily, many treasurers will, sensibly enough, just mail you the list. Indeed, in some counties in Nebraska, you can even get a list with pictures of the properties!

Occasionally treasurers—thankfully not many—make this first step difficult. Because bidding at the auction requires your personal appearance, and because you need to spend some time checking out the properties anyway, you probably won't mind picking up a list when you get there.

Checking Out the Properties

The process of locating the best residential areas where liens are available and of determining which properties are adequately improved is described in chapter 9 ("Getting Local Officials to Help You"). Without repeating those instructions, I will add that because you are physically in the county, you should take advantage of that by visiting the neighborhoods and at least some of the properties that are on the list.

No matter how enthusiastic the other bidders are about a property at the auction, that does not mean that they know anything about it. Don't follow a blind leader. If you have checked out a property to your own satisfaction, let it pass.

Checking in at the Auction

Some states have elaborate protocols for registering at the tax lien auction. For example, at the auction in Miami, Florida, you must register in advance and give the tax collector a form containing your Social Security number. You will then be given a buyer number. You must then pay a $1,000 deposit, which you will get back in about a month if you buy no certificates. For each additional day you show up, you must deposit 10% of the cost of the purchases you made the day before. Other counties require that you estimate the amount you will buy and deposit 10% of that.

How Do You Bid?

The lowest bid, then, is the winning bid. The auction is, in effect, held as sort of a favor to the delinquent property owner.

In most states, the amount of money you are going to pay to get a tax lien certificate is exactly the amount of the delinquent taxes, plus the interest and penalties already owed to the county by the property owner. What you are bidding for is the amount of interest you are going to require the property owner pay to you.

Therefore, if the highest rate of interest allowed in that state is 18%, the first bid on the property is 18%. If another bidder wanted that tax lien, he would have to agree to accept, say, 17¾% interest. The lowest bid, then, is the winning bid. The auction is, in effect, held as sort of a favor to the delinquent property owner. If the tax lien on his property is not sold at the auction, he will owe the maximum rate of interest.

Not all states work this way, however. In Colorado, for example, the tax lien certificate goes to the person who pays the taxes, interest, and penalties owed, *plus* the largest amount of cash. The cash goes directly into the county's general fund. The property owner gets no benefit from the auction in Colorado, and the bidders can never be sure in advance how much money they will need to pay to get a certificate.

In Maryland, you bid the amount you are willing to pay for the property. All you must pay at the time of the auction, however, are the taxes due. The rest must be paid when and if you ever get a final decree giving you the property.

In Michigan, the tax lien certificate goes to the bidder who agrees to take the least undivided interest in the property should there be no redemption. In that event, the lucky winner will be a tenant in common with the delinquent property owner!

When Do You Pay?

Each of the states is very specific about when you owe the money and how you must pay it.

In Arizona, the entire amount of the bid must be paid in cash or check at the time of the sale. Wyoming says that the county treasurer must be paid "immediately." There is no room for fudging here.

In Florida, by contrast, you must give the tax collector 10% of the money due, or some higher figure set under local procedures. After your certificate has been prepared, if you do not pay the rest of the money within 48 hours, you lose your deposit.

Other places require payment by the next day, or before the conclusion of the sale. If you fail to show up, the tax lien is merely auctioned off again.

Tactics at the Auction

There is really only one variable at the auction, and that is the intensity of the competition.

At one auction in Miami, for example, 13,500 certificates were available, more than enough for the handful of buyers attending the auction. For that reason, no one bothered to bid less than the 18% maximum rate of interest. One investor said: "Why should I take 17% when I don't want all of them?"[1] The year before, however. there was more of a crowd, because bank interest rates were lower.[2]

At a well-attended auction, the rates may be bid down unreasonably low.[3] For this reason, if you have a choice you should consider auctions in less popular and populated counties. There are no invariable rules, however. In one recent year, only 25 bidders attended the tax lien sale in Palm Beach.[4] Three years later, there were still only 60 attendees.[5]

In the current economic climate, you will see more interest in tax lien auctions because of the low prevailing interest rates. At the same time, because of the continuing recession, there are plenty of tax lien certificates on the market.

It will be a pretty good year.

Can You Deduct the
Trip to the Auction?

As a general matter, no deduction is allowed for travel expenses for investigating new investments.[6] On the other hand, if you are the holder of substantial investments in tax lien certificates, and you take a trip to buy more, an argument can be made that you are in the "business" of buying tax lien certificates, and that therefore your trip is deductible.[7] As a general rule, however, investors are not in a trade or business and cannot deduct expenses of obtaining investments as business expenses.[8]

Even if you are not in the "business" of buying tax lien certificates, however, your expenses related to buying the certificates are not lost forever. For tax purposes, expenses connected with acquiring an investment are added to the cost of the investment (in tax language, this total cost is the investment's "basis").[9] When it is time to pay taxes, the higher your expenses, the lower your taxable gain. And even if you are not in the "business" of buying tax lien certificates, once you have the certificates, travel expenses spent in looking after your investments (for example, arranging for foreclosure) will be deductible.[10] These deductions, however, are among those deductions which must exceed 2% of adjusted gross income before they do you any good. They are also subject to decrease for high-income taxpayers.[11]

Notes

1. "Buyers Rush to Invest in Delinquent Tax Bills." *Miami Herald,* p. 14BR (June 2, 1983).

2. Ibid.

3. Spear, "Banks, Thrifts Getting in on Tax-Certificate Game." *Orlando Sentinel,* 2 Star Section, p. 1 (May 28, 1988).

4. Tolpin, "Tax Collector Auctions Certificates on $37 Million in Delinquent Taxes." *Palm Beach Sentinel*, Local Section, p. 38 (June 15, 1989).

5. Smith, "Annual Tax Certificate Sale Under Way—Low Risk Investing." *Palm Beach Post*, Business, p. 5B (June 4, 1991).

6. 1992 Prentice Hall Federal Tax Course, 2000(e), p. 2004.

7. Ibid.

8. Federal Tax Coordinator 2nd L-111 (1992).

9. Internal Revenue Code, 1012.

10. Federal Tax Coordinator 2nd. L-1400 et seq.

11. U.S. Master Tax Guide, 1012, 1013.

CHAPTER 7
Armchair Values in "Leftovers"

[T]he whole point of an auction is to place you in competition with others, in order to reduce your profit.

Why Buy Direct From the Tax Collector?

As you will discover when you attend your first tax lien auction, they are interesting and exciting and profitable. You will make new friends and pick up tips from pros. But remember, the whole point of an auction is to place you in competition with others, *in order to reduce your profit.* But what if there were a way you could bypass this process and get the maximum interest that the state allows? You can.

The fact is, there are billions of dollars in available tax liens spread over more than 1,200 counties in 27 states. There have always been more tax liens than demand from tax lien investors. Not at every time and at every place, but always and in many places.

Several states have laws which specifically provide that if a tax lien does not sell at the auction, you can then go directly to the county tax collector and buy it. You do not need to bid against anybody. The interest rate will be the highest possible. You do not even have to physically go to the tax collector's office. This is as close to ideal as investing gets.

In some states, the rush for unsold certificates can be greater than at the auctions. In Michigan, for example, after the first year of delinquency, the interest rate goes up to 50%. Further, because of a strange feature of Michigan law, if you buy at the auction you could end up as a co-owner of the property along with the delinquent owner. This causes the tax collector's offices to be popular just before the second year rolls around.

You must, of course, check to be sure that the county you pick has leftover liens, and indeed that the state you pick allows direct purchases after the auction. Some states, like Iowa, provide that if any leftovers exist, they will be auctioned off at another time.

Tips on Buying Direct

Try the Smaller Counties

The major drawback in buying directly from the tax collector is that you may only buy what was not bought by anyone else at the auction. This certainly means that the selection is less, and it could mean that there are no available properties at all in that county, or at least none that you want.

In my experience, this is not a problem. Still, your chances of finding good direct buys is greater in the more rural counties, where the auctions draw far fewer people.

Buy Early in the Year

Whenever you buy a tax lien certificate, you must pay the treasurer not only the back taxes, but also whatever interest and penalties have accrued up to that time.

There is no real disadvantage in this, so long as the tax lien certificate is actually redeemed. In fact, you will be earning interest on this larger amount of money. But if the property is not redeemed, and if you can eventually turn in the tax lien certificates and be handed a deed for the property, any extra amount you pay for the certificate is coming out of your own pocket, because you could have gotten the same property for less.

Establish a Relationship with the Local Officials

The system I prefer for buying tax lien certificates depends upon relationships with county employees working in places which are not always easy to get to. Most businesses depend, at their root, upon personal relationships and this one is no exception. In chapter 9 ("Getting Local Officials to Help You"), I explain my system in detail.

CHAPTER 8
Buying from Other Investors

By now you know that tax lien certificates are a spectacular investment. But what if you could buy them at a discount?

[M]any of the failed thrifts have sizable portfolios stashed away, ignored.

Bargains in Tax Lien Certificates from Other Investors

By now you know that tax lien certificates are a spectacular investment. But what if you could buy them at a discount?

Ask George Baur of St. Petersburg, Florida. He bought a collection of tax lien certificates from the Resolution Trust Corporation (the government agency which takes over ailing savings and loan associations). He paid some $835,000 for certificates worth over $1 million, when the interest is factored in.[1] Some 600 properties back up that package, and when two years go by from the time the failed thrift bought them, Mr. Baur can foreclose the liens. The underlying property is worth up to $40 million.[2]

This is just the tip of the iceberg. James McNamara, the president of a New Orleans–based tax consulting firm, notes that tax lien certificates were listed as approved investments for thrifts, and that many of the failed thrifts have sizable portfolios stashed away, ignored.[3] One of the reasons many were ignored is that some failed thrifts had not cataloged or managed what they had, and did not know when to foreclose on the properties, or in some states, when to simply walk in and ask for a tax deed.

The RTC has been unable to inventory—let alone manage—the incredible collection of assets which it has under its control. If you have the time and the patience to deal with an overwrought and sometimes surly bureaucracy, some impressive bargains are possible. And some of them are in tax lien certificates.

The RTC is far from your only source of bargains. You will recall that in chapter 3 ("How Do Tax Lien Certificates Fit Into Your Investment Plans?"), I discussed a negative point about tax lien certificates: their lack of liquidity. Because there is no organized private market for buying or selling tax lien certificates, it is possible that some investors who had not expected to need the money before cashing in their certificates now feel differently. Finding a distress sale, whether through word of mouth or through advertisements, may be more of an effort than simply buying a certificate from a county, but it may be worth it.

Just remember, regardless of the source of your certificates, whether from the county governments, the RTC, or private investors, you need to check out the properties before you buy them, as I explained in chapter 4 ("Selecting an Area") and chapter 5 ("What to Look for in Properties"). Of course, if you are getting a huge and fabulous grab bag of certificates like Mr. Baur did, and you don't mind if the certificates are of varying value, you can make an exception.

Finding a distress sale, whether through word of mouth or through advertisements, may be more of an effort than simply buying a certificate from a county, but it may be worth it.

Managing Liquidity Through Relationships

The search for a bargain is not the only reason why you might be interested in the transfer of tax lien certificates. You might decide to join with one or more investors and buy tax lien certificates in the same area, with an understanding that if one of you needs to cash out, the others will pick up the certificate.

Such an arrangement not only provides extra liquidity, but can make for some good vacations as well, as you travel to your favorite tax lien–selling resort with your friends.

How to Transfer Tax Lien Certificates

States that sell tax lien certificates have provisions specifically allowing you to assign a certificate to another person. An assignment is, after all, how you got your lien from the county in the first place.

The illustration on the next page shows the back of a typical tax lien certificate. Notice that on the left side of the certificate, the county assigned the lien to you. On the right side, the certificate is blank, awaiting your assignment to someone else.

Just because you fill out this form does *not* mean that the certificate is effectively transferred. At this point, the county would know nothing about the sale. If the tax lien certificate is redeemed, the county would assume that the person who bought it still owns it, and would pay the redemption money to that person.

For this reason, it is of vital importance that the transfer of the tax lien certificate be registered with the county. This usually requires that the tax lien certificate be sent to the county, and may require a nominal fee, for example $1.00 in Florida.

Notes

1. "The Grapevine." *Thrift Liquidation Alert*, p. 6 (May 20, 1991).

2. Ibid.

3. "Tax Liens Lure Savvy Investors." *Thrift Liquidation Alert*, p. 3 (February 20, 1991).

CHAPTER 9
Getting Local Officials to Help You

Breaking the Gibberish Barrier

You have now read chapters 4 and 5. You have decided what states you want to consider for your tax lien investments, and you know what kinds of properties you want to target. Three years ago, you made the trip to Arrowhead County for the tax auction, but right now you are looking for some of those "armchair values in 'leftovers'" I described in chapter 7.

You pull out your copy of the local newspaper that listed the properties that had been available for this year's auction. The list is not too informative. It begins:

PARCEL NO.	OWNER	DLQ TAX
145–02–00700	Lefoe, Manny & Freda	427.06
145–02–00975	DuPres, Charles Q.	381.12
145–02–01765	B & Q Builders	967.53
145–03–00276	Futheng, Hans & Bertha	476.98
145–04–01987	FBN PRESS	1,254
146–01–00145	Bigelot, Norma	767.50
146–01–00568	Lupis, Jan and LeRoy	2,187.75
146–02–00986	Second Story Title	1,347.32

Obviously, you have no idea what these parcels look like, where they are, or what might be on them. Any of them could already have been sold at the auction, and some could have been bought just afterward for the full interest rate. It's time to call in Ethyl.

No, I don't mean that you need a higher grade of gasoline. I mean Ethyl, the Deputy County Clerk. And really, I don't mean my Ethyl. She's my secret. You need to find your own Ethyl. I will tell you how.

You mail the list to Ethyl with a note asking her which parcels are still available. She sends your list back. Ethyl has circled 15 of the properties. Time for a call to Frank at the County Assessor's Office.

What you need from Frank is a breakdown on the assessments to show how much is allocated to the land and how much to the improvements on these properties. If the land's assessed value is more than 40% of the total assessment of the property, this is a situation you should skip. In a couple of minutes, you have 11 good properties.

Now here is where Ethyl really helps beyond any call of duty. You don't know where these properties are, and for that matter, you know nothing about the county in which you are buying. Ethyl does. First, though, you need to take the time to chat with her. She is, after all, living in a small town, in an office where there is plenty of time to chat. She asks about your boy John, who just applied to college, and tells you about her niece's wedding last weekend. It seems hard to believe that you met Ethyl only one time.

You do turn the conversation around to neighborhoods. Ethyl mentions the tax lien certificates on Wintergreen Heights. She says that this is a resort area where there are many second homes. It's at least as nice as Copper Corners, where you have been buying. "In fact," she says, "just about everything in Book 146 is good."

After a little while, you tell her which five properties you want. The last thing you need to know is exactly how much the interest and penalties have added up to on these properties since the time of the auction. She tells you, and you reply that you'll get a check out to her today. You talk a little longer, and you tell her you'll call in a few weeks.

Today is the 15th of the month. If you get your check out today, she'll be sure you get the interest for a full month (that's an extra $150 for every $10,000 you're investing at 18%!). If you didn't know Ethyl, the clerk might only allow your interest to start running the month after your check cleared, or wouldn't accept your personal check at all.

Finding Your Own Ethyl

Sound too good to be true? In many places, it is. In Dade County, Florida, for example, the clerks are so busy that the local rules require you to somehow figure out for yourself how much money is owed on a property, let alone where it is and what might be on it.

Your answer is simple: focus on the less populated rural counties. In many of these places, life is slow and your Ethyl has the time and the inclination to be neighborly. Besides, in a small town, your Ethyl will know every neighborhood, if not every block, and will be pleased to share what she knows.

Another advantage of shopping for tax lien certificates in a rural county is that there is much less competition. While scores of people may show up for a tax lien auction in Denver or Orlando, greater bargains may be available in a smaller city with no bidding down at all from the maximum rates of interest.

To establish the kind of relationship I am describing, it is likely that you will have to limit the number of counties in which you are investing. This is certainly no hardship. In my experience, even the smallest county will have more qualifying properties ready for your investment than you are likely to need.

If at all possible, begin your relationship in person. This is not to say that you cannot establish fast friendships entirely by phone. Still, these things are much better done in person. Besides, the better you know an area, the more comfortable you will feel with your investments, and the more enthusiastic you are likely to be about the possibility of obtaining property in the area at a bargain price.

If you do call, keep in mind that the person who handles tax lien sales might go by different names in different states. In some states, the county auditor handles the sales; in others, the treasurer does this; in still others, you must ask for the tax collector. (For the prime states detailed in appendix 2, I tell you which office to request.) You should also know that not all states refer to the sales as tax lien sales. In Mississippi, for example, the sale is called the land tax sale.

To establish the kind of relationship I am describing, it is likely that you will have to limit the number of counties in which you are investing.

Ethyl is not going to be too popular with at least one property owner in her county if she helps you into a position where you can foreclose on property.

Nothing can really take the place of personally inspecting each property. Still, having Ethyl's help comes mighty close.

When you find your Ethyl, no matter how helpful Ethyl is, you must not, of course, become a pest. When you call, you should be very specific about what you are looking for, and you should have done your homework by reviewing all the information you have available, including the procedures used by the state, as described in appendix 2.

There is some basic political etiquette you have to respect. Ethyl is not going to be too popular with at least one property owner in her county if she helps you into a position where you can foreclose on property. Particularly if you are not a resident in her county, you can't help her boss be reelected or reappointed. She will not mind assisting you in finding and paying for tax lien certificates, because the local voter would have been liable for the same interest and penalties anyway. Still, mentioning foreclosure is about as welcome as mentioning malpractice to a doctor.

You can ask her which areas have the highest redemption rates and which have the lowest. Nevertheless, when you casually chat, you must be a person after a high rate of return. And as a practical matter, that's what you are.

Nothing can really take the place of personally inspecting each property. Still, having Ethyl's help comes mighty close.

SECTION 3
How to Get Your Money or the Property

CHAPTER 10
How to Redeem Your Certificates

CHAPTER 11
Foreclosing on Tax Liens

CHAPTER 12
Managing and Marketing Foreclosed Properties

CHAPTER 10
How to Redeem Your Certificates

Not much needs to be said on the subject of redeeming tax lien certificates, because one of their nicest features is that the work of processing a redemption is done for you by the local treasurer.

If the property owner decides to pay off the lien, he does not contact you. Rather, he goes to the treasurer's office and pays the delinquent taxes, as well as the penalties and interest. In some states, he gets a "certificate of redemption" in return for this, which he can record. In most places, he just gets a receipt.

Next, the treasurer goes to the records to see who gets the money. In places where you will be keeping the original tax lien certificate, a notice will go out to you that the property has been redeemed, and that you should send in the certificate. After the treasurer receives the certificate, he mails you a check. In places where the treasurer keeps the original certificate on file, he just mails you the check. You should be aware that some time could pass here if the treasurer's office is busy. You will be earning no interest at all during this period.

In a few states, such as Michigan, you will also need to sign a "quitclaim deed," in which you acknowledge that you have no further interest in the property.

In order to fully appreciate the ease and comfort of this arrangement, you need to have invested in, for example, second trust deeds. There, you not only have to worry whether you are adequately secured, but you have to establish a relationship with the debtor, check his credit, take his payments, listen to his sad stories. With tax liens, the treasurer provides all these services for free. Best of all, unlike second trust deeds, you do not even care whether you are paid off, because you would be more than happy to get the property free of senior mortgages in return for the few cents on the dollar you have invested. In the case of a second trust deed, you would

One of life's best financial events is when you get a check in the mail much larger than the one you wrote to get your tax lien certificate.

still have to pay off the senior lender, which could cost you thousands or even hundreds of thousands of dollars.

At this point, I must give you a reminder that at the time you change your address, you must go through your tax lien certificates and put the treasurers on your list of people whom you notify. The best way to do this is in a letter which lists the parcel numbers and your certificate numbers, and which requests that the records be changed to reflect your new address. Any other owners of your certificate should also sign the letter.

It is not at all unusual for property owners to wait two years or longer before redeeming the property. By that time, if you moved, the Post Office may have stopped forwarding your mail and you would have no way of knowing of the redemption. The amount of interest lost in this transition can be considerable because, of course, once the property is redeemed, no one is paying you interest on your certificate. Even worse, if you fail to claim the money in a reasonable time, which is sometimes fixed by statute, you may lose your rights to it!

One of life's best financial events is when you get a check in the mail much larger than the one you wrote to get your tax lien certificate. And you know that your getting this check is not the result of luck, as with the stock market, but is something you can do again and again.

Take a moment to congratulate yourself. But do not rest on your laurels. Remember that this check represents not only your success, but also that you are no longer earning that high interest rate on these funds. The figures I gave you showing that you can earn over $1 million on a single $2,000 deposit requires that you keep that money hard at work for you. If you let it snooze in a money market account until you can get around to recycling it into another tax lien certificate, your returns are going to be dramatically less.

CHAPTER 11
Foreclosing on Tax Liens

The sun is just sinking behind the New York skyline, as lights are appearing all over the city and on the boats cruising the river. No matter how often Jim sees this from his New Jersey riverside condo, he thinks it is the best show in town. And his next thought is that if his condo wasn't the best buy in town, he doesn't know what was. Just $10,000 in tax lien certificates got him this $200,000 place! And his other tax lien certificates have bought him the time to retire and enjoy it. Not bad for 49 years old. Life is just beginning again.

As though the super-high interest rate of tax lien certificates were not enough, they sometimes bring an extraordinary bonus. That a foreclosure on a tax lien does not happen every day will, like winning a lottery, increase the thrill when it does happen.

The first thing to understand about tax lien foreclosures is that every state has its own peculiar requirements. Some states require you to post a notice of the foreclosure in three public places; others require none. Some state require you to run advertisements for four weeks, some for two, some for none. Even if you know the procedure perfectly in one state, it will mean nothing in another.

The second thing to understand about tax lien foreclosures is that the law is strict about procedures. Any failure to follow the required process may stop you from getting a deed to the property, or may make any deed you do get void. This is a time to be precise.

It is also, in my opinion, a time to get a lawyer. I say this with some bias, because I am a lawyer. But there is a lot at stake here, and the costs of a lawyer are easily justified. If you get the property, you'll be getting it for pennies on the dollar. And if the debtor pays up during the process, *he* will generally have to pay your attorney's fees. Besides, in most states, you are going to have to go to court, where you will have to file pleadings and present evidence. Any mistakes may result in your case being thrown out. The judge, who does not know you, is unlikely to cut you any slack. This is no time to be cheap. When I am in this kind of situation, I hire local counsel.

In appendix 2, I review the foreclosure requirements in several states. In this chapter, I will review the features that are common to all states.

Notice of Foreclosure

All states require that before you foreclose on property, you must give notice to those interested in the property.[1] This is not only a requirement of state law, but also of "Due Process" under the federal Constitution.[2] The statutes nonetheless vary in their details concerning what the notice must contain, who gets notified, and how.

The person who is listed on the property records as the owner of the property must receive notice of the foreclosure. Often, the law will require that persons actually on the property must be notified, too.[3] This is sensible and fair, as those persons could hold a long-term lease which is about to be wiped out. Further, mortgage holders must be notified.[4] Courts have held that among the parties entitled to notice are heirs of the property owner and other parties holding tax lien certificates.[5] This last notification is not strictly relevant as to holders of other tax liens, because in many states, you are required to pay off these lienholders before foreclosing. Even were you not so required, you must as a practical matter pay off other tax liens, or the holders of these liens could simply foreclose on your title.[6] The notice to mortgage holders will often trigger them to pay off your lien, because if the foreclosure goes through, their mortgage will be wiped out.

If the property owner is known and can be located, "personal service" is most often required. This involves hiring a process server to personally deliver the notice. Each statute will specify when service by certified or registered mail should or must be made.

All states allow "service by publication," that is, notification in a specified newspaper, to substitute for personal service if the person to be served cannot be located.[7] Although absolutely no one looks through the legal notices to see if maybe some item applies to him, the law pretends that everyone does. Often, the state law requires publication in a newspaper even if you have personal service, just in case some unknown person might have an interest in the property.

You cannot get too cute about notification. In one case, a lienholder gave notice in the English language, in a newspaper printed in a foreign language, apparently thinking that the owner would surely not be browsing through *that* newspaper. The court threw the notification out.[8]

The courts can get extremely technical even where no tricks are being played. One line of cases in Missouri holds that the use of initials in the notice is invalid where the property owner uses his full name on the deed.[9]

Some states require posting on the property and/or public places as part of the notice procedure.

The notice must adequately describe the property to be foreclosed. If it does not, the notice is no good, and the court lacks jurisdiction.[10] This means that the property owner or the mortgage holder can attack your deed even if they do not appear at the foreclosure proceedings. In addition, the notice must say when and where the proceedings are to be held, the name of the owner of the land, and the kind of taxes due.[11]

If notice is not properly given to some person, but he shows up at the proceedings anyway, the failure to give good notice is waived.[12]

Do You Have to Go to Court?

Not every state requires you to go to court to foreclose on a tax lien. Some states allow you to apply directly to the tax collector for a tax deed. A few states, such as Arizona, give you a choice. In that state, if you want to foreclose after three years, you have to go to court. However, if you don't mind waiting five years, you can apply directly to the tax collector for a deed.

In general, and even though it is a lot of bother, you are better off going to court, because the people who will be buying the property from you, or issuing title insurance on it, will feel a lot better if you have a court judgment saying that the property is yours.

In fact, I feel so strongly about the assistance that a court judgment gives you that I advise you to bring a "quiet title" action (a proceeding in court asking that you be declared the true owner of the property) even in cases in which you did not need to go to court to get your deed.

What Happens in Court?

What the judge is interested in is whether your papers are in proper form, and whether they recite all of the facts required for you to be entitled to foreclose, including the required notification of the proceedings.[13]

Sometimes the property owner will come in and argue that the foreclosure should not take place. Occasionally, he is right, such as when he can prove that he really paid the taxes, but did not get proper credit. A claim that the property was assessed too high, however, comes too late, unless he can prove that this was some sort of fraudulent scheme to make him lose his property.

Most of the time, though, the proceedings are "default," meaning that no person opposing the foreclosure appears.

What Do You Get from the Court?

What the court proceedings result in differs from state to state. In most states, the tax collector or some other official is ordered to issue a deed.[14] In Florida, all you get is an order that the property be sold to the highest bidder, and you are allowed to bid in the value of your tax lien certificate, plus the interest you have earned.

What About Taxes?

You did it! You've landed what may be the best bargain of our life! Go ahead and cheer; go out and celebrate. But tomorrow, hire a tax lawyer.

Odd as it may seem, there is no regulation clearly covering whether foreclosing on a tax lien and getting the property is a taxable event. If it is, you will owe income tax on the difference between the value of the property and the cost of the tax lien. If not, you will pay tax on your gain when you sell the property.

At this point, you should protest that all you did was get some property at a bargain price. If I sell you my new $20,000 car for $1,000, you hardly owe income tax on your $19,000 "gain." A tax will be owed only when you sell the car for more than you paid.

The IRS has a regulation, however, that says that if "mortgaged or pledged" property is "bought in" by the creditor for less than the value of the property, then gain is realized in the amount of "the difference between the amount of those obligations of the debtor which are applied to the purchase or bid price of the property . . . and the fair market value of the property."[15] The idea behind this regulation is that because the creditor will be able to deduct a bad debt if the property is sold for less than the mortgage,[16] he should be required to declare a gain if the property brings the creditor more than the mortgage.

Of course, in the case of tax lien certificates, we are not talking about "mortgaged or pledged property." Nevertheless, you may need to argue about whether you owe the tax upon foreclosure, or rather upon sale of your new property.

With a little planning, this should not be too much of a problem. First, you can control when the foreclosure occurs. Plan on foreclosing early in the year, so that you have time to sell the property before the end of the year. That way, if you do owe a tax, you will have the money to pay it. Second, market the property right away. Having bought it cheap, you can afford to offer someone else a relative bargain for a quick sale. You should take these actions regardless of tax issues, in order to keep your funds earning at tax lien rates.

No question, taxes are annoying, and uncertainty in taxes is doubly annoying. Still, it is better to have gained and been taxed than never to have gained at all.

Notes

1. 85 Corpus Juris Secundum, Taxation, 740.

2. 72 American Jurisprudence 2d, State and Local Taxation, 916.

3. Ibid., 914.

4. Ibid., 897.

5. Ibid.

6. Ibid., 965.

7. Ibid., 928.

8. Ibid., 916.

9. Ibid., 922.

10. Ibid., 915, 919.

11. Ibid., 918.

12. Corpus Juris Secundum, 740.

13. American Jurisprudence 2d, 741.

14. Ibid., 973.

15. IRS Regulation 1.66-6(b).

16. IRS Regulation 1.66-6(a).

CHAPTER 12
Managing and Marketing Foreclosed Properties

Congratulations! You have hit a home run in the tax lien game. You have a property which is worth from 10 to 50 times what you paid for it. You are, quite rightly, thrilled.

What should you do now? I, for example, have some tax lien certificates on second homes in mountain resorts. Should I get one of those properties, I'm going to keep it. For the most part, though, our investment cycle is not complete until we translate our new property into cash.

Selling a property which you acquired through foreclosure of a tax lien is similar to selling property that you acquired any other way. There are, however, some special factors to consider and some points worth stressing.

Get Liability Insurance

As a very first step, call an insurance agent in the area of your new property and get liability insurance. You are now the owner of the property, and people will be coming through it. You have no real idea of what condition it's in. Protect yourself. And while you're about it, get fire insurance too. You have no lender to remind you and to require this. However, you now have an investment to protect.

Consider a "Quiet Title" Action

Second, even though you have the title, you should consider bringing a "quiet title" action. This is a lawsuit brought against any potential claimants to the property, in which you seek a declaration from the court that you hold good title. This court judgment will help protect you against any later legal challenges to your title by persons who think that they were not given the required notice, that the description of the property was not adequate, etc. The person who buys the property from you is going to want to be assured that she is getting good title. She is not trying to buy a lawsuit with the former owner. Likewise, a title insurance company may require you to do this.

Bring Any Necessary "Unlawful Detainer" Action

Just because you now have legal title to the property does not necessarily mean that the former owners or any tenants/ guests/squatters have left or have any desire to leave. As the new owner, you could be in a position similar to that of a landlord whose tenant is not paying the rent. Your solution is an eviction or "unlawful detainer" action.

An unlawful detainer action seeks an order from the court granting you possession of the property. Once you have that order, you can seek the assistance of the sheriff in removing the inhabitants and their possessions.

In many states, an unlawful detainer judgment can be obtained in a matter of weeks. It proceeds faster than a "quiet title" action. Still, if you believe that the inhabitants are going to mount a serious challenge to your title, you may want to combine the unlawful detainer and the quiet title actions, even though the case will proceed slower.

However you proceed, you cannot put things off for too long, because the inhabitants of your property may, after a period of years, attempt to claim title to the property through "adverse possession," sometimes called "squatter's rights," and the law of the state may back them up if you sleep on your rights past the statute of limitations.

Obviously, these decisions are not a do-it-yourself project, even if you happen to be familiar with the state's laws and the county's procedures. Visit a local attorney. One nice thing about having acquired the property as cheaply as you did is that you have a vast amount of equity and have every incentive to do things correctly and thoroughly.

Price the Property Aggressively

In most parts of the country, we are past the "go-go" years when everyone had access to a fortune merely through owning real estate. Your newly-acquired property has to compete as an investment with the alternative of your selling it and reinvesting the proceeds in more tax lien certificates. As you have just experienced, that's tough competition for any alternative investment. You would have to clear at least 16% per year, even after expenses, through not selling. This is unlikely.

In every investment, many who begin well but do not fully succeed have fallen prey to the "piggy factor." They push a good thing too far and have to pay the price. You have a lot of equity in your new property. Consider pricing the property low for a quick sale.

Pay the Taxes!

I know it sounds bizarre, but some folks who get the property through foreclosure on tax lien certificates fail themselves to pay the property taxes! The prior owner has just given you a vivid object lesson. Learn from it.

SECTION 4
Avoiding and Managing Risk

CHAPTER 13
"Worthless" Properties

Why the Taxes Weren't Paid

"There's usually a reason the taxes aren't paid," an article in *Forbes* hints darkly.[1] Actually, there could be several.

At least initially, the reason may be simple forgetfulness. Harry Knight, the tax collector of Monroe County, Florida, observed that most delinquent accounts are caused by negligence. "They put it off and put it off, and then they wake up."[2]

A most common reason is that the owner simply does not have enough money for the taxes. Or, the money for the taxes may be there but the owner may not be able to pay the mortgage, and figures that it is not worth paying the taxes just so the bank, rather than the tax collector, takes the property.

Occasionally, the owner believes that he has such a great use for the money that causing the county to make an involuntary loan is worth the interest and penalty he must pay. As an example of this last reason, Earl K. Wood, the tax collector for Orange County, Florida, asked a prominent local businessman who turned up on his list of delinquencies each year why he didn't pay on time. "Earl," he replied, "it's cheap money."[3]

Every once in a while, a property owner concludes that the property is simply not worth the taxes. Sometimes, he is right. As *Forbes* points out, "It could be something on the side of a mountain, or wetland, or zoning restrictions may not permit you to build on it."[4] An additional possibility, one covered in the next chapter, is that the property has an environmental problem.

How do you sort out the worthless properties from the gems?

. . . the tax collector for Orange County, Florida, asked a prominent businessman who turned up on his list of delinquencies each year why he didn't pay on time. "Earl," he replied, "it's cheap money."

*[In Florida],
"$10,000 in
assessed tax-lien
value probably
would buy a
15-acre lake
full of rocks or
a small plot on
which you could
put a billboard,
if you're lucky."*

Avoiding Worthless Properties

Check the Assessments

One of the excellent features of tax lien certificates is that each property comes with a free professional appraisal of its market value by a government agency.

True, the appraisal can be wrong, but if it is grossly wrong the owner had every incentive to appeal the assessment, because the taxes owed were based on the appraisal. Leaving the appraisal unreasonably high, and then forfeiting the property because the property is not even worth the taxes, would be a wholly illogical reaction.

Relate the Appraised Value to Appraised Values in the Area

If the assessment appears to be unreasonably low for the area, you should not deal with the property until you have explained the discrepancy. For example, if the property is supposedly improved, but the improvement is appraised at $15,000, you have to assume that there is something wrong with the property or that the structure has only salvage value, in which case it would have to be demolished before you could make any use of the property.

Your aim in checking the assessments is to find an appraised value which appears to be no lower than the appraised values of properties in the area. If it is much lower, it's more likely that there is something wrong with the property than that you have found a great bargain.

In making this comparison, you need to consider the general values in the area of the country where you are dealing. An improved property in a small town in Arizona might be just fine with an appraised value of $40,000. A similar property in urban Connecticut would likely be a disaster.

For example, Richard Gardner, the assistant tax collector for Dade County, Florida, said that in his area, "$10,000 in assessed tax-lien value probably would buy a 15-acre lake full of rocks or a small plot on which you could put a billboard, if you're lucky."[5]

Stick With Improved Properties

The rules of wise real estate investing apply to the selection of tax lien certificates. One of the most important of those rules is that raw land is a much more difficult investment to check out than improved land. Because you are buying a tax lien certificate rather than the property itself, and are (or ought to be) buying several certificates on different properties, you need to deal with properties which are easy to evaluate.

For the most part, a property has market value because of what can be done with it. Improved property has proven that it has some use; raw land requires a good deal more investigation. The following are but a few of the factors that stand in the way of raw land ever being developed:

Zoning: One of the most obvious reasons that raw land might not ever be improved is that the local government will not allow improvement. This need not be so crude as zoning the property as "Open Space." Zoning a property as residential in the middle of a heavy industrial area will make economic improvement very difficult. Often, there is very good reason why development is restricted, such as that the land sits atop an old dump or that a major earthquake fault runs through it.

When deciding on an investment in raw land, zoning should be the first thing you check. Nor should you stop there. If the county has a general plan, you should look at that too. It shows not only what the uses of the surrounding land are projected to be, but also what the zoning of the land you are investigating may soon be.

Flooding: One summer night 25 years ago, I was driving toward Yosemite National Park when I spotted by moonlight the most beautiful acre of land I had ever seen. The Merced River glistened as it flowed by a white sand beach. Pine trees ringing the land swayed softly in the breeze. I had to have it for a cabin.

. . . raw land is a much more difficult investment to check out than improved land.

The next day, I went to the county recorder's office and explained the location of the land. After a time, the men in the office got a look of recognition, and then burst out laughing. "That is a fine looking piece of land, son," one of the men chortled. "We go fishing there pretty often. But in early spring, it's under 10 feet of water!" I knew then that I had a lot to learn.

If you are seriously considering raw land near water, you had best go to the local Planning Department and see what areas have been designated as floodplains. Next, visit the history section of the local library and try to learn what areas were washed out by big floods.

True, improved land can flood too. But if the improved land is in a neighborhood of improved properties, a lot of people are betting that the improvement will not be washed away. And if the improvement is still there, this is some proof that the property is safe.

While seemingly arid lands can often be served by wells, not every property is above usable groundwater.

Water Rights: Just as bad as land that floods is land with no access to water. Unless the land is served by a water agency, and that agency confirms that it stands ready to serve this land, you need to provide your own water.

Particularly in the dry Western states, access to a reliable water supply is not assured. If you visit a property in spring and see a merry creek gurgling through the property, it is as likely as not that, should you return in September, you will see a dry ditch.

While seemingly arid lands can often be served by wells, not every property is above usable groundwater, and determining what water is available and who else is laying claim to it can be an expensive and time-consuming process.

Sewage Disposal: In developed urban areas, we take sewage disposal for granted. While building your house, you merely hook up to the sewage line that runs down the street.

In many areas, however, there may not be a sewage line, and you are faced with wondering whether the property percolates sufficiently so that a leach field can be installed.

Because you typically do not have access to a property to

perform a leaching test before you invest in a tax lien certificate, you are faced with guessing about the geology of the site from the experience of neighbors, if there are any.

Beware of Phony Improvements

Aaron was thrilled. He had been investing in tax lien certificates for three years, but had never actually foreclosed on a property before. Now he had, and was the proud owner of land improved by a residence in a residential development. Proudly, he drove across the state to see the property he had gotten so cheaply.

When Aaron turned around the last bend in the road leading to the property he saw . . . nothing at all! A visit to the local general store revealed that the "residence" was nothing but a mobile home, and that, while the neighborhood was zoned for a great many more mobile homes, the development had never taken off; but the owner of the property had—with his mobile home! The property was, by itself, almost worthless.

If I have persuaded you to stick with improved properties, your next task is to be sure that the supposed improvements are real. In the above story, which is entirely true, and all too common, the residential neighborhood was worse than a ghost town; at least in a ghost town, the buildings are left behind.

Be Friends with the County Clerk

In chapter 9, "Getting Local Officials to Help You," I advised you that the surest way to get tax lien certificates on the best properties is to get a local government employee to steer you to where the best properties are.

Most cities have areas where you wouldn't want to be walking after dark. Some counties have entire towns where you would not want an interest in property. Times Beach, Missouri, comes to mind. It was charming; it had a picturesque setting by the Mississippi River; it was a lovely place, except for the detail of its being contaminated by dioxin, and

Some counties have entire towns where you would not want an investment in property.

You only need to sell your property to one person.

thus ordered abandoned by the EPA. One town I dealt with as California's toxic waste chief was literally built on deposits of hazardous waste. When my staff tried to warn the residents, they replied hostilely that this was just a "plot" by the next town to annex them.

Problem areas, or even problems with individual properties, are best known by local people. If you are not a local person yourself, it would be a good idea to make the acquaintance of one.

Diversify

Despite all of your precautions, you may eventually meet up with a property that is not even worth the small amount of your tax lien. It is at this time that you lick your wounds and console yourself with the thought of the huge returns you made on the tax lien certificates that paid off for you.

Look for Hidden Value

In one case with which I am familiar, someone bought a tax lien on an unbuildable strip of land between two nursing homes. Surely, it was useless—except to one of the neighbors.

You only need to sell your property to one person. While it would be fine if a property on which you hold a tax lien certificate were universally appreciated, and while you should definitely seek out properties that are, if you break all the rules and end up in a tight spot, this could be your opportunity to project yourself in the position of potential buyers with special needs.

Notes

1. Lebove, "Caveat Emptor." *Forbes,* p. 80 (December 24, 1990).

2. Nelson, "Tax Collector Is Ready to Lien on Tax Arrears." *Miami Herald,* State Section, p. 18 (September 8, 1983).

3. Snyder, "How to Make a Profit Paying Someone Else's Taxes." *Orlando Sentinel*, Business, p. 1 (April 29, 1990).

4. Lebove, supra, quoting George Szydlowski, a Connecticut tax lien investor.

5. Kendall, "Investment Network Targets Area Poor, Promises 'Control of Money.'" Vol. 8, *The Business Journal of Milwaukee*, Sec. 2 p. 3 (January 28, 1991).

CHAPTER 14
Environmental Problems

What Problems?

The Good News

For over 20 years, I have been an environmental lawyer, first with the government, and for the past seven years with a large international law firm. Based on my knowledge and experience, I can deliver the good news—that buyers of tax lien certificates can avoid environmental liabilities.

Because the rules of environmental liability are often not understood, discussions of real estate–based investments, including tax lien certificates, are often accompanied by vague warnings about environmental problems.

One avid investor in tax liens gave the following observation to *The Business Journal of Milwaukee:* "If you purchase a tax-lien certificate and it turns out to be environmentally contaminated, it could cost you all the other property you own."[1] *The Thrift Liquidation Alert* says that "investors in tax liens are warned to examine underlying properties carefully to determine whether they are environmentally flawed—a factor that could make foreclosure a losing proposition if cleanup costs are high."[2] *Forbes* notes: "Finding you have a tax lien on the local Love Canal won't do you much good."[3]

Almost any investment imaginable can be done wrong. But if you follow the basic rule I discuss in this chapter—stick with residential property—you will not be kept up at night by this issue any more than you are about the environmental safety of your own backyard. Those of you who intend to buy tax liens on residential property may skip this chapter. For those with more exotic properties in mind, this chapter is for you.

The Bad News

The bad news is that those who do suffer environmental liabilities can suffer badly. A congressional agency estimates that cleaning up contaminated properties will cost over $1 trillion. The average cost of cleaning up a single property on the EPA's "Superfund List" is $30 million.

A common misunderstanding is that government funds will clean up this problem. In fact, the federal cleanup program has been given $8.5 billion to spend over five years. Some simple arithmetic will tell you that it would take hundreds of years for this money to do the job.

An even more common misunderstanding is that the "polluters" are being forced to clean up their messes. While this does occur, in fact, over a long period of time, only about 5% of cleanup money has come from the polluters.

Instead, Congress decided that individual owners and lessees of property should bear the cost of cleanup, even if they did not cause the pollution and had no idea that it was there.[4] This astonishingly unfair idea has been plaguing real estate transactions ever since, and has spawned new classes of consultants and expenses. In one famous, but happily rare case, a man who bought a building for $380 in back taxes was later informed by the Environmental Protection Agency that the property was contaminated and would cost between $600,000 and $1,000,000 to clean up. He was even threatened with a fine of $25,000 for each day he failed to clean up the property.[5]

Two solutions are available to you as a buyer of tax lien certificates: the "physical solution" and the "legal solution." The "physical solution" refers to those simple actions that you should take before getting involved with a property, actions that make it much less likely that the property is polluted in the first place. The "legal solution" refers to actions you must take to get the advantage of a special exemption that Congress has provided to lienholders, including holders of tax lien certificates. In this chapter, I will tell you in detail how to protect yourself in both of these ways.

Two solutions are available to you as a buyer of tax lien certificates: the "physical solution" and the "legal solution."

... it [is] not physically or financially possible for you to send every grain of sand to a hazardous materials laboratory to be absolutely sure that the property of choice is not contaminated.

The "Physical Solution"

Your Best Protection: Stick with Residential Properties

In chapter 5, "What to Look for in Properties," you learned that improved residential properties are your best choice if you are looking for a tax lien that will likely be paid off, and if you want property which presents excellent security for the loan. This same advice holds true for avoiding environmental problems.

Even if you were a professional real estate investor, it would not be physically or financially possible for you to send every grain of sand to a hazardous materials laboratory to be absolutely sure that the property of choice is not contaminated. Professional investors therefore select properties which present a minimum possibility that hazardous substances are present. Using that criterion, the property of choice is residential property.

This is not to say that residential property is *never* contaminated. The infamous Love Canal in New York, for example, where startled property owners began seeing industrial wastes seep into their basements, is a residential community. As an extreme example, in one case I worked on a couple moved deep into the woods in order to flee civilization, only to find that the land around their rustic cabin had been polluted by the former owner, who made his living salvaging old transformers. Only a volunteer cleanup organized by California's toxic substances control chief (me) saved this couple from financial ruin. Particularly in rural areas, gasoline tanks may have been installed near homes, and those tanks are sometimes leaking today. Likewise, in some communities, underground heating oil tanks are common, and these must be considered to be leaking until proven otherwise.

Still, with some exceptions, the possibility of residential property being contaminated is so rare that almost no buyers of residences, nor their even more cautious lenders, pay much attention to it.

If you are cautious, you should ask whether the neighborhood has always been residential. Often you will learn that it had previously been farmland. This presents some possibility that the farmer had been overenthusiastic with his use of pesticides. Still, as the property was graded, this problem is often diluted below any level of concern, and the passage of time certainly helps break down many pesticides. As a practical matter, former farmland should not cause worry.

Occasionally, you will learn that the neighborhood is redeveloped industrial land. This would be a good property to skip. While the chances are good, particularly if the development is recent, that the developer or the lender checked out the property and that a report by an environmental engineer exists, you do not normally have the time to evaluate this situation in detail in order to buy a tax lien certificate.

For Higher-Risk Properties: The "Phase 1" Investigation

If you stick with buying tax lien certificates on residential properties, the odds are you will never have environmental problems. Still, fabulous opportunities exist in tax lien certificates on commercial properties. Particularly if your aim is to acquire the properties, you may be considering commercial properties. I would then suggest that you do what professional lenders and investors do in this situation and have a "Phase 1" environmental evaluation performed.

A "Phase 1" evaluation is designed to confirm that hazardous substances have never been present on a property. It begins by asking about the history of the property. A sample questionnaire is included for your use in appendix 3. It is typical of information that an environmental consultant will want to review before beginning a "Phase 1" investigation. Once the questionnaire is complete and reveals no history of the presence of hazardous substances, the remainder of the investigation usually consists of at least the following three steps:

1. A trained environmental consultant will walk through the property, looking for signs of environmental problems, such as discolored soil, sickly vegetation, or vent pipes, which indicate the probable presence of underground tanks.

2. Government records will be searched to see if the property is on one of many lists of contaminated properties, or if a permit for underground tanks had ever been issued for the property.

3. Historical aerial photographs will be searched to see what the use of the property was over the past several decades.

Other techniques are less often used, such as searching title records to see if the property had an owner with an "industrial-sounding" name.

One problem may be obvious: the chances are not good of your consultant being allowed to conduct a walk-through inspection on private property (unless the property is open to the public). You may have to settle for what observations you can make from a legal vantage point, and perhaps redouble your efforts at a record search, for example by pulling all old business permits issued on a commercial property.

You can expect to spend at least $3,500 for a "Phase 1" survey. The investigation will require about three weeks. For around $500 more in most parts of the country, you can (and should) hire an environmental lawyer to supervise the investigation. The lawyer can often hire the consultant for less, giving you two experts for the price of one. Further, the lawyer will save you from the worst parts of contracts often used by consultants. Finally, the lawyer will catch and fix problems with draft reports (such as the tendency of some consultants to recommend more work for themselves) and will help preserve the confidentiality of the report.

For those of you who reject the above commercial for lawyers, I have also included in appendix 3 a form contract which you may use in place of your consultant's form contract. Many other forms are found in my book, *Environmental Liability and Real Property Transactions* (John Wiley & Sons).

"Phase 1" investigations are very popular, as they are relatively quick and inexpensive. When they bring trouble, it is because they are used in an inappropriate situation. As I mentioned, the purpose of a "Phase 1" investigation is to confirm that hazardous substances were never present. If the investigation reveals that hazardous substances *were* present, the "Phase 1" has been flunked, and I suggest you pass.

As is clear from this discussion, a "Phase 1" investigation is not reasonably possible in order to invest in most tax lien certificates. Nor is it necessary, if you stick with residential properties.

For Highest-Risk Properties: The "Phase 2" Investigation

The only way that you can tell whether hazardous substances were released at a property where they *were* present is to send representative samples to a laboratory. This process, logically enough, is called a "Phase 2" investigation.

In my experience, when a property requires a "Phase 2" investigation, it should be considered to be a risky investment. In many cases it is hard to know where to take a sample, or what to sample for. One thing you can be sure of is that a property which requires a "Phase 2" investigation will be sharply more expensive to check out.

The problem of obtaining access to the property is magnified in the case of a "Phase 2" investigation. This may not be just a lack of friendliness or desire to have little holes poked in the property, or to discourage a possible tax sale. The fact that an environmental consultant is visiting the property may concern the owner that the investigation could reveal a problem, causing a bigger headache for him than the failure to pay back taxes.

... the purpose of a "Phase 1" investigation is to confirm that hazardous substances were never present. If the investigation reveals that hazardous substances were present, the "Phase 1" has been flunked, and I suggest you pass.

The "Legal Solution"

When Congress passed the so-called "Superfund Act,"[6] it made all "owners and operators" of property liable for contamination on the property, whether they caused the contamination or not. Lenders were worried. They held liens on property as security for loans. In some states these mortgages were considered to be the technical "ownership" of the property.

According to the EPA, the exemption from cleanup liability for lienholders is not lost just because there is a foreclosure on the lien.

In order to avoid being required to clean up the property, lenders persuaded Congress to give lienholders a special exemption from liability. This exemption said that a lienholder is not an "owner or operator" so long as the lender is acting "primarily to protect his security and interest in the property" and so long as the lender is not "participating in the management" of the facility.[7]

Over the years, there has been much discussion in legal circles over exactly when a lender is acting "primarily" to protect the loan, and exactly what actions can be taken without "participating in management." The limitations on this exemption are of no concern to an investor in a tax lien certificate before there is a foreclosure on the property. A tax lien certificate gives no right to "participate in management" in any way. Further, the only function of a tax lien certificate is to protect the security interest.

What if the taxes and penalties are not paid and you end up owning the property outright? Do you lose your lienholder's exemption? The EPA gave a comforting negative answer to this question in regulations issued in June 1992,[8] but unfortunately those rules were overturned in court. Still, they may have some value as general guidance.

According to the EPA, the exemption from cleanup liability for lienholders is not lost just because there is a foreclosure on the lien. If the property is then auctioned, the protection of the exemption is not lost just because the lienholder then obtains the property. There is one exception to this, though: If the lienholder outbids, rejects, or fails to act within 90 days on a written, legally enforceable and reasonable cash offer, the protection is lost and the lienholder/owner will be responsible for cleaning up the property if it is contaminated.[9]

Because tax lien certificates usually represent only a small percentage of a property's value, in those states that require an auction it is very rare for a reasonable offer to be less than the amount of the lien, and therefore very rare for a person bidding only the amount of a tax lien certificate to outbid a full-price reasonable offer.

According to the EPA's former regulations, once you have the property, if you want to keep the lienholder's exemption, you must try to sell the property. As to how hard you have to try, the EPA said that you must either list the property within 12 months following the foreclosure with an appropriate broker, or else advertise the property in an appropriate publication at least monthly. In either case, you must accept the same written, enforceable, reasonable cash offers which you would have had to accept at an auction.[10] Even if you do not follow these rules, if the EPA decided that you tried reasonably hard to sell the property, you would keep the exemption.

If the property has an ongoing business on it, the EPA's former regulations would allow you to maintain the ongoing business activities while keeping the exemption.[11] However, if you proceed to contaminate the property yourself, you should not expect an exemption from liability.

While these rules are simple to follow, there are some cautions:

First, environmental laws change quickly, and the cases interpreting them change even quicker. The disappearance of the EPA's regulations is a good example.

This is not to say that there need be anything wrong with deciding to keep the property and thereby losing the protection of the lender's exemption. However, if you plan to hold on to a property, you should also hold on to the exemption while you check it out with the same care as though you were buying it on the retail market, using the guidelines for "Phase 1" and "Phase 2" investigations discussed above.

Using the investigation guidelines in this chapter and your own common sense make tax lien certificates as safe as any real estate investment.

. . . if you plan to hold on to a property, you should also hold on to the exemption while you check it out with the same care as though you were buying it on the retail market . . .

Notes

1. Kendall, "Investment Network Targets Area Poor, Promises 'Control of Money.'" Vol 8, *The Business Journal of Milwaukee*, Sec. 2, p. 3 (January 28, 1991).

2. "Tax Liens Lure Savvy Buyers." *Thrift Liquidation Alert*, p. 3 (February 25, 1991).

3. Lubove, "Caveat Emptor." *Forbes*, p. 80 (December 24, 1990).

4. Joel S. Moskowitz, *Environmental Liabilities and Real Property Transactions* (John Wiley & Sons, 1989, and Supp. 1992).

5. Mark L. Manoil, "Lien Risks Involve Liquidity, Security, Litigation." *Arizona Business Gazette*, International Trade Section, p. 18 (February 3, 1994).

6. The legal name and citation of this act is the Comprehensive Environmental Response, Compensation and Liability Act, 42 U.S.C. 9601 et seq.

7. 42 U.S.C. 9601(20)A.

8. 57 Fed. Reg. 28798 (June 5, 1992).

9. 57 Fed. Reg. at 18262; 40 C.F.R. 300.1100(d)(2)(ii).

10. 57 Fed. Reg. at 18384; 40 C.F.R. 300.1100(d)(2)(i).

11. 57 Fed. Reg. at 18366–67, 18284; 40 C.F.R. 300.1100(d)(2).

CHAPTER 15
Bankruptcy

One objection to tax lien certificates that is occasionally raised is that the property owner may declare bankruptcy. For example, *Forbes* darkly reported:

> Among the booby traps awaiting investors: a bankruptcy filing by the delinquent taxpayer that wipes out the lien-holder's claims—even though a tax lien is superior to all others . . .[1]

To call this unclear is kindly. It is nonsense.

The short answer, for those who cannot stand suspense, is that you will be OK. You, as the holder of a tax lien certificate, are a secured creditor, and a senior creditor. Further, you are a creditor whose lien is almost always a small fraction of the value of the property. You can get your money, with interest, out of this investment.

The major downside of a bankruptcy filing is that it will almost certainly delay your ability to foreclose on the property, sometimes by a few years.

You need to be alert if you get a notice of bankruptcy. You may need to file a claim. However, handled correctly, a declaration of bankruptcy is a bump in the road—an inconvenience, but rarely a disaster.

Because this is a subject of some concern, I will briefly summarize the bankruptcy laws and how they apply to tax lien certificates.

. . . handled correctly, a declaration of bankruptcy is a bump in the road—an inconvenience, but rarely a disaster.

Three Types of Bankruptcy

Bankruptcy commonly comes in three forms: Chapter 7, Chapter 11, and Chapter 13. These names refer to the chapters of the Bankruptcy Code which govern these proceedings.

Chapter 7

Sometimes called "straight bankruptcy" or "liquidation bankruptcy," Chapter 7 can be used by either individuals or businesses. The proceedings may be voluntary, or may be compelled by creditors.[2]

In either case, a trustee is appointed.[3] The trustee's job is to pursue any rights the bankrupt's estate may have, to avoid any liabilities that can be avoided, and to distribute whatever is left to creditors according to priorities established in the law.[4]

A debtor may elect Chapter 7 proceedings to receive a "fresh start," using whatever assets are exempt from transfer to the creditors. A business will use Chapter 7 as a way to dissolve in an orderly manner.

Chapter 11

Chapter 11 is sometimes called "reorganization bankruptcy." Almost always, the debtor remains in possession of the property and functions much as a trustee would, pursuing remedies and avoiding liabilities.[5]

A committee of unsecured creditors, and sometimes additional committees, are appointed.[6] These committees investigate the debtor's financial situation, and attempt to work out a reorganization plan.[7] During the first 120 days, the debtor has the exclusive right to propose a plan.[8] If the court orders otherwise, or the 120 days pass, then others, including the creditors, may propose a plan.[9]

The reorganization plan might provide for the payment, over time, of some or all of the debts. It could, however, call for the liquidation of the business.[10]

The creditors will hopefully agree to the plan. If certain classes of creditors disagree, the plan may be imposed over their objections, under some circumstances. This is known as a "cramdown." In either case, if the plan is confirmed by the bankruptcy court, it will govern the rights of the creditors thereafter.[11]

Chapter 13

Unlike Chapters 7 and 11, a Chapter 13 bankruptcy can be used only by individuals, and it may only begin voluntarily.[12] Further, the individual needs to have a regular income, if only from welfare.[13] For this reason, a Chapter 13 bankruptcy is sometimes known as a "Wage-Earner's Plan."

A Chapter 13 can only be used by smaller debtors; those whose unsecured debt is $100,000 or less, and whose secured debt is $300,000 or less.[14]

While a trustee is appointed in Chapter 13 cases, he is usually the same trustee who handles all Chapter 13 cases in the district. The debtor remains in possession of his property.[15]

The debtor alone can propose a Chapter 13 plan. The creditors do not even get a vote.[16] Creditors with no special priority need not, and often do not, get anything under the plan.

A Chapter 13 plan commonly lasts for three years, although it may be extended for two more.[17] It calls for the debtor to pay his disposable income to the trustee, who will distribute it to the creditors according to the requirements of the plan. Unlike a Chapter 7 or 11 case, the debtor's obligations are not immediately discharged; rather, the debtor's reward for carrying out the plan is to have the court discharge all debts not satisfied through the plan after the debtor completes the payments under the plan.[18]

A debtor may satisfy a secured creditor in a Chapter 13 plan by: (1) paying the debt over the life of the plan, (2) allowing the creditor to keep the lien and make payments equaling the present value of the debt, or (3) turning the collateral over to the creditor.[19]

If the debtor does not follow the plan, the Bankruptcy Court can dismiss the case, convert the case to a Chapter 7 bankruptcy, or discharge the debts anyway on the ground of hardship.[20]

There are several nuances of difference between these forms of bankruptcy, but this summary will suit our present purposes.

... the most important effect of the filing is the immediate and automatic freeze on any actions by creditors to enforce their claims ...

The Automatic Stay

Imposing the Stay

Regardless of which type of bankruptcy is chosen, the most important effect of the filing is the immediate and automatic freeze on any actions by creditors to enforce their claims outside of the Bankruptcy Court.[21] Indeed, a most frequent reason for the filing of bankruptcy is to obtain an automatic stay on a foreclosure by a secured creditor.

The effect of the automatic stay does not depend upon whether you know of the filing or not. Once the bankruptcy case is filed, any action taken contrary to the automatic stay is given no legal effect, and indeed must be undone.[22]

Once a bankruptcy petition is filed and until the bankruptcy is discharged, the automatic stay is lifted, the property is no longer in the bankruptcy estate, or no action can be taken to enforce a lien on the property,[23] including the foreclosure of a tax lien certificate.

Lifting the Stay

To ask that the stay be lifted for "cause" will generally require you to show that the debt is not adequately protected . . .

Once an automatic stay is in place, there are only two reasons why it might be lifted to allow a secured creditor to foreclose: (1) because the debtor has no equity in the property anyway, so lifting the stay will not affect the distribution of property in bankruptcy, or (2) for "cause."[24] To ask that the stay be lifted for "cause" will generally require you to show that the debt is not adequately protected (meaning that your interest will be somehow harmed by the continuation of the stay).

In most cases, lack of adequate protection for a secured creditor means that the value of the property may not be adequate to cover the value of the claim, and that this value might deteriorate further. This is sometimes referred to as the lack of an "equity cushion."[25] In the case of a tax lien certificate, where the amount of the debt is usually only a small fraction of the value of the property, it is rare that you can argue the lack of an "equity cushion."

In cases where there is not adequate protection for the secured creditor's debt, the Bankruptcy Court will fashion some protection, such as periodic payments to offset the deterioration in value, or else a lien on other property.[26] Even if there is an adequate "equity cushion," where the secured creditor is financially hurt by the continuation of the stay, and where lifting the stay will not harm the debtor or the other creditors, the Bankruptcy Court may decide to lift the stay.[27]

"Exempt" Property

Certain types of property are exempt from the reach of creditors in bankruptcy proceedings. Examples are tools of one's trade, health aids, household goods, and a homeowner's exemption in real property.[28]

The exemption of certain property is not of concern in the case of tax liens, however, because a tax lien, notice of which is properly filed, is not subject to exemptions.[29]

"Avoidance" of Transfer by Trustee

Preferential Transfers

A bankruptcy trustee has the power to cause to be set aside any transfer of property within 90 days of the filing of bankruptcy that preferentially pays one creditor over another of the same class.[30] For example, if a creditor pays a debt owed to his lawyer before declaring bankruptcy, the trustee can set this transfer aside, even though the debt was bona fide.

A trustee may not, however, set aside a transfer made pursuant to a valid statutory lien.[31] To be a statutory lien, the lien must be one which would exist regardless of the pendency of bankruptcy, or of the debtor's financial condition. Further, it must be a lien which could be asserted against a bona fide purchaser of the property (i.e., one who had no actual knowledge of the lien). Finally, it must not be in favor of a landlord for rent.[32]

A property tax lien, evidenced by a tax lien certificate, fits these requirements: One owes property taxes whether one is

. . . should you foreclose on a tax lien certificate, after which the property owner declares bankruptcy, your foreclosure is not subject to being set aside as a preference.

rich or poor, and whether one is in bankruptcy or not. Because tax obligations are of record, a new buyer of a house could only buy a house subject to the tax lien; the mere sale would not wipe out the lien whether the buyer had actual knowledge of the unpaid taxes or not. Finally, tax liens do not involve a landlord collecting rent. Therefore, should you foreclose on a tax lien certificate, after which the property owner declares bankruptcy, your foreclosure is not subject to being set aside as a preference.

The foreclosure of a tax lien will often result in the holder of a tax lien certificate receiving a property worth far more than the taxes owed. Still, this does not disadvantage other creditors, because the certificate holder would have that right regardless of whether there was a bankruptcy or not, and regardless of what actions other creditors might take.

Fraudulent Transfers

A bankruptcy trustee can set aside a "fraudulent transfer" made within one year before the bankruptcy filing.[33] Where property is bought at a foreclosure sale for less than the supposed fair market value, there are some cases which suggest that this was a "fraudulent transfer," even though it involved no collusion with the debtor, and even though it makes little sense to talk of the market value of the property as being more than the price actually paid. Other cases disagree.[34]

While this theory seems absurd, that does not mean that some trustee will not try to use it, or that some bankruptcy judge will not accept it. The Bankruptcy Court is widely known as the "Wild West" of legal tribunals, where results are as often achieved with elbows and bluster as with careful legal reasoning.

The result of setting aside a foreclosure sale is that the property will be returned to the estate, and the lien will be restored.[35]

Filing a "Proof of Claim"

The major difference, for our purposes, between the types of bankruptcy is that in Chapter 7 and Chapter 13 cases, se-

. . . in Chapter 7 and Chapter 13 cases, secured creditors need not file proofs of claim . . . while in Chapter 11 cases they must do so if their claims are not properly listed or recognized.

cured creditors need not file proofs of claim, although under some circumstances they may want to do so, while in Chapter 11 cases they must do so if their claims are not properly listed or recognized.

Thus, in a Chapter 7 case, only unsecured creditors must file a "proof of claim."[36] This rule has no application to the holder of a tax lien certificate, because the claim is secured by the property.[37]

In a Chapter 11 case, the debtor prepares a list of claims and interests in his property. Any person whose claims or interests are listed in the proper amount, and whose claims and interests are not described as disputed, contingent, or unliquidated (i.e., are in a presently unknown amount), does not need to file a proof of such claims and interests.[38] The creditor's filing must be made before a date set (and which can be extended) by the Bankruptcy Court. This date is known as the "bar date."[39]

In a Chapter 11 case, you are in worse shape if the debtor puts down your lien for the wrong amount than if he never lists you at all. There is authority that if you are absent from the debtor's list, your lien will survive the Chapter 11 proceeding even if you do not file, but you will be bound by errors in the debtor's listing.[40] Because you will not usually see the debtor's list, the sensible course will be to file a proof of interest in the proper form before the bar date, attaching the tax lien certificate.[41]

In a Chapter 13 case, as in a Chapter 7 case, a secured creditor need not file a proof of claim unless the claim is challenged.[42]

Collection of Interest After Filing of Bankruptcy

Where the property is worth more than a secured claim, the creditor is entitled to interest on the claim. The property securing a tax lien certificate is almost always worth far more than the taxes due. You will therefore be entitled to interest on the debt.[43] This interest may not, however, be at the same rate you were earning under state law.[44]

. . . the possibility that a property owner will go into bankruptcy is a manageable risk.

Putting It Together: Dealing With Bankruptcy

We can conclude from this discussion that the possibility that a property owner will go into bankruptcy is a manageable risk. So long as a timely proof of claim is sent to the Clerk of the Bankruptcy Court in a Chapter 11 case, the investment is secure. You do not even need to do this in a Chapter 7 or Chapter 13 case. The automatic stay will delay your foreclosure until the bankruptcy is over, but you could meanwhile get some interest.

All things considered, you would rather not deal with a property that is tied up in a bankruptcy. Therefore, if you happen to know that a property owner is or will be in bankruptcy, you should stay away from a tax lien on the property, because the bankruptcy will reduce your liquidity.

Checking the Bankruptcy Court files in the owner's district of residence is a possible caution. On the other hand, the owner could always declare bankruptcy after the sale.[45] Considering the overall statistical and tactical risk posed by bankruptcy, and the number of properties you will be dealing with, this level of diligence may not be cost-effective.

Notes

1. Lubove, "Caveat Emptor." *Forbes*, p. 80 (December 24, 1990).

2. 11 U.S.C. 301–303.

3. Ibid., 701–703.

4. Ibid., 726.

5. Ibid., 1107.

6. Ibid., 1102.

7. Ibid., 1103.

8. Ibid., 1121.

9. Ibid.

10. Ibid., 1121.

11. Ibid., 1129.

12. Ibid., 303(a), 706(c), 1112(d).

13. Ibid., 109.

14. Ibid.

15. Ibid., 1306.

16. Ibid., 1321.

17. Ibid., 1322(c).

18. Ibid., 1328(a).

19. Ibid., 1322(b).

20. Ibid., 1328(b).

21. Ibid., 362, 922.

22. R. Ginzberg, Bankruptcy: Text, Statutes, Rules ("Ginzberg"), pp. 198–199, 3.01[b][1] and [2] (1989 and 1991 Supp.).

23. 11 U.S.C. 362(a)(3)–(5).

24. Ibid., 362(d).

25. Ginzberg, supra, p. 248, 1305[e].

26. Ibid., p. 247, 3.05[d][1].

27. Ibid., pp. 252–253, 1305[f].

28. 11 U.S.C. 522.

29. Ibid., 522(c)(3); 5 Collier, Bankruptcy Practice Guide ("Collier"), p. 74–78, 74.02[5] (1992).

30. Ibid., 547.

31. Ibid. 547(c)(6).

32. 11 U.S.C. 545.

33. Ibid., 548.

34. Ginzberg, supra, pp. 694–696, 9.03[g]; 2 Cowans, *Bankruptcy Law and Practice* ("Cowans"), p. 219, 10.9.

35. 11 U.S.C. 548(c).

36. Fed. Rules of Bankr. Proc. 3002(a).

37. 11 U.S.C. 548(c).

38. Ibid., 1111(a).

39. Fed. Rules of Bankr. Proc. 3002(a).

40. L. Lopucki, *Strategies for Creditors in Bankruptcy Proceedings*, p. 731, 12.7 (2nd Ed. 1991).

41. 5 Collier, supra, pp. 88-21–88-23, 88.11[3][c] (1992).

42. Ginzberg, supra, p. 779, 10.07[e].

43. 11 U.S.C. 506(b); 2 Cowans supra, p. 602, 12.32 (1991) [involuntary lien entitled to interest].

44. Ibid., p. 606, 12.32.

CHAPTER 16
Scams

Considering the fabulous legitimate opportunities presented by tax lien certificates, and the relative ease of purchasing them, it would seem improbable that they would be fodder for consumer fraud. At least it would seem improbable until one reflects on the endless ingenuity of con artists and the equally endless gullibility of their victims.

In the case of tax lien certificates, the high value represented by the properties coupled with the low cost of the investment creates a "spread" which is ripe for a creative sales pitch.

So it was that in Milwaukee a fellow named Melvyn gathered together members of the Hmong refugee community and invited them to join the International Loan Network for a mere $225. This cost allowed them to become a "Daddy Tom" and get part of similar fees paid by new recruits. According to their own estimates, some 40,000 people have joined this group.[1]

For another $400, you get the right to join the "$1,000 Property Rights Assignment Program," which entitles you (if you pay an additional $250 processing fee) to have assigned to you a tax lien certificate on property with an assessed value of no less than $10,000.[2]

That might sound good for half a second, until you reflect that the last tax lien certificate I bought cost me $1,300 and the assessed value of the property was $40,000. This would seem to mean that the lien on the $10,000 property could easily have cost the promoters $325!

If you like that investment, though, you would love the opportunity to pay $5,000 for a tax lien certificate on property assessed at over $50,000, or a $10,000 certificate on property assessed at over $100,000. Naturally, the additional "processing fee" on these bigger transactions is raised to $500.[3]

Odd as this deal is, apparently 162 people in Milwaukee bought tax lien certificates this way on property that they knew nothing about. One tax lien investor rightly called this buying "a pig in a poke."[4] An expensive pig at that.

The Securities and Exchange Commission took an interest in this plan and obtained a preliminary injunction. It told a United States court of appeals that this pyramid scheme violated securities laws and that the sales were made without adequate disclosures.[5]

Obviously, if you are reading chapter 16 of this book, you would not have gotten caught up in such a plan. There is no "entry fee" needed to buy tax lien certificates, and no need to vastly overpay for them. So this chapter is not so much a warning as something for us to marvel at together.

When tax lien certificates enter the mainstream of investment interest, no doubt regulations specific to them will follow, as is the case with stocks, bonds, mutual funds, and commodities. At the moment, the best that can be said is that if you don't buy your tax lien certificates directly from the government, having done your own homework, then delegate the buying only to a person you trust entirely and verify through the county treasurer that what you are buying is genuine.

This is hardly to say, of course, that delegating the time and bother of investigating and buying the certificates has no value. True, the experienced tax lien investor who commented on the International Loan Network said: "Why pay someone else to do something you can do yourself at no cost?"[6] I suppose that means that his wife cuts his hair. There is plenty of reason to pay people to do things you *could* do yourself. Just make sure you pay the right people the right price for the right article.

No doubt, the next development in tax lien investments will be the proliferation of local buying services, and on a larger scale limited partnerships and even mutual funds. Already one limited partnership is functioning in New Jersey and Maryland. A fully developed market will save you time and will give you access to professional managers and record-keepers. This will be a convenience and a welcome development. And it will almost certainly be a better bargain than the International Loan Network.

Notes

1. Kendall, "Investment Network Targets Area Poor, Promises 'Control of Money.'" *The Business Journal of Milwaukee,* (January 28, 1991).

2. Ibid.

3. Ibid.

4. Ibid.

5. Bureau of National Affairs, "SEC Urges Appeals Court to Affirm Injunction in ILN Investment Scheme." 24 Securities Regulation and Law Report 683 (May 8, 1992).

6. Kendall, *supra.*

CHAPTER 17
FDIC/RTC Liens

Lawyers have a saying: "Hard cases make bad law." The crushing expense of bailing out the savings and loan and banking industries has led the two federal regulatory agencies, the Federal Deposit Insurance Corporation (FDIC) and the Resolution Trust Corporation (RTC), to take the position that their liens cannot be wiped out by foreclosure without their consent.

The situation that most often arises does not involve tax liens. It comes about like this: a savings and loan funds a second mortgage on a house. Later the savings and loan becomes insolvent, and is taken over by the RTC. When the senior lender tries to foreclose, the RTC claims that the foreclosure cannot take place without its consent.

The RTC's legal support for this position is questionable. The statute on which it relies (nicknamed the "consent statute") says:

> No property of the Corporation shall be subject to levy, attachment, garnishment, foreclosure or sale without the consent of the Corporation, nor shall any involuntary lien attach to the property of the Corporation.[1]

This statute is clearly designed to apply to the property owned by the agency. The assertion that its lien is the "property" referred to here is farfetched. The RTC nevertheless says that "[p]roperty of the Corporation encompasses any interest in . . . property . . . including security interests as well as any equity interests."[2]

Another argument, which is seemingly inconsistent with this last one, is based on a statute (nicknamed the "redemption statute") which expressly allows the United States to be named in a suit "to foreclose a mortgage or other lien upon . . . real . . . property on which the United States has or claims a mortgage or other lien."[3] In such a case, however:

[t]he United States shall have one year from the date of sale within which to redeem . . .[4]

The interest paid upon this redemption, however, is only 6%.[5] The statute requires, moreover, that the foreclosure of the government's junior lien be at a "judicial sale."[6]

Needless to say, lenders were not one bit happy about the application of the "consent statute" and the "redemption statute" to themselves. Several of their associations joined together to complain, including the American Bankers Association, the Federal National Mortgage Association, the Mortgage Bankers Association, the U.S. League of Savings Institutions, and the National Council of Community Bankers. They urged the RTC and FDIC to assert these statutes only in cases involving state and local tax liens.[7]

The RTC responded with an "interim policy statement" in which it consented to foreclosure of "voluntary" liens.[8] What the RTC means by a "voluntary" lien is any lien that the property owner agreed to, such as the mortgage lien he agreed to place on his property in order to get his loan.

Nevertheless, the RTC reserved a right to require its specific consent in the case of foreclosure of "involuntary" liens. These liens were not agreed to by the property owner, but are imposed by law. Examples given are tax liens, mechanic's liens, and judgment liens. At the same time, the RTC indicated that in no case would it assert its right to a full year to redeem following foreclosure.[9]

The RTC is not arguing that a foreclosure of a senior lien without its consent is void. Rather, it says that such a foreclosure will not wipe out the RTC's lien.[10] The implication is that if a senior lien is foreclosed without the RTC's consent, then the interest conveyed by the sale is junior to the RTC's lien.

The RTC says that it wants requests for consent to be delivered at least 30 days before the date of the foreclosure sale. The notice must specify the time, date, and place of the sale and the manner in which it will be conducted. Finally, the notice must state the name of the institution for which the RTC has been appointed the receiver. The RTC will send that request to its asset manager, who is supposed to determine

The RTC is not arguing that a foreclosure of a senior lien without its consent is void. Rather, it says that such a foreclosure will not wipe out the RTC's lien.

As of now, the courts have not decided the validity of the RTC's position that its "property" includes liens that it is managing.

"within thirty to sixty days" (it may take longer) whether the RTC's lien has any value, and whether it is in the RTC's interest to grant consent.[11]

As of now, the courts have not decided the validity of the RTC's position that its "property" includes liens that it is managing, and that neither local governments nor private parties holding senior liens from local governments under state law can foreclose on these liens without the RTC's consent. The question is being litigated in a state court in Texas, and some attorneys who have studied the matter have concluded that federal agencies such as the RTC will only be allowed to step into the shoes of the thrifts that they take over and have no better rights.[12]

What does all this mean to you?

First, when the owner of the property is the RTC or the FDIC (or any other federal agency, for that matter) this would be a good tax lien certificate not to buy.

Second, when you know that the RTC or the FDIC has taken over a thrift which holds a mortgage on a property, you will do better to avoid a tax lien certificate on that property.

Third, if you plan to foreclose on a tax lien certificate you already own, check who the lender is, and check whether the lender has been taken over by the FDIC or the RTC. If you discover that it has been, hold off on foreclosing on the tax lien unless you want to try to obtain the agency's consent. It will do you little good to own a property subject to the assertion of the RTC or FDIC lien, and you can hardly afford to litigate this sort of dispute, given the small amount of money you are likely to have at risk.

Fourth, if you nevertheless find yourself in the situation of having a tax lien certificate on a property with a lien managed by the RTC or FDIC, do not despair. Not even the expansive position of the RTC goes so far as to suggest that a junior RTC lien wipes out a senior tax lien. Indeed, it does not and cannot. Nor will the existence of an RTC or FDIC lien stop your accrual of interest. Nor will the RTC see any value out of the property unless you are first paid off, with interest. Special care must be taken, however, in states which require foreclosure in a short period of time, such as two years in Maryland

and three years in Iowa. This can create a dilemma where awaiting resolution of the federal lien issue could push you over the state's deadline for foreclosure.

In summary, the RTC might prevail in court, and this is an issue worth noting. However, it is an issue that with some care concerns liquidity, and not the safety of your investment. It is another reason for diversifying your investment among a number of properties.

Notes

1. 12 U.S.C. 1825(b)(2).

2. 57 Fed. Reg. 19651, 19652 (May 7, 1992).

3. 12 U.S.C. 2401(c).

4. Ibid.

5. Ibid., 2410(d)(2).

6. Ibid., 2410(c).

7. BNA, 58 *Banking Report Thrift News* 137 (January 27, 1992).

8. 57 Fed. Reg. at 19652–19653; BNA, 58 *Banking Report Thrift News*, 829–830 (May 11, 1992).

9. Ibid.

10. Ibid., at 19653.

11. 57 Fed. Reg. at 19654–19655.

12. Dialog File 148, *Trade and Industry Index*, ISSN 1895–1551 (1992).

Appendices

APPENDIX I
Chart of State Laws

APPENDIX II
The 16% Winner's Circle

APPENDIX III
**Environmental Forms
for Commercial and
Industrial Properties**

APPENDIX IV
Further Information

APPENDIX I
Chart of State Laws

State	Rate of Interest	Redemption Period	# of Counties	Notes
Alabama	6%	3 years	67	
Arizona	16%	3 years	15	Foreclosure a little easier after 5 years
Colorado	fluctuates	3 years	63	9% above federal discount rate
Florida	18%	2 years	67	
Georgia	10%	1 year	159	
Illinois	18%+	2½ years	102	
Indiana	10%–25%	1 year	92	
Iowa	24%	1¾ years	99	Foreclosure required in 3 years
Kentucky	12%	3 years	120	
Louisiana	17%	3 years	64	Rate is 12% after first year
Maryland	varies	2–6 mos.	23	Foreclosure required in 2 years Baltimore pays 24%
Massachusetts	14%–16%	2½ years	14	
Michigan	15%–50%	12–18 mos.	83	Foreclosure required in 5 years 50% is second year's rate
Mississippi	17%	2 years	82	
Missouri	10%	2 years	114	
Nebraska	14%	3 years	93	
New Hampshire	18%	2 years	10	
New Jersey	18% + 2%–6%	2 years	21	Foreclosure required in 20 years
New York	10%	2 years	62	Only in some counties
North Dakota	9%–12%	3 years	53	Foreclosure required in 10 years
Oklahoma	8%	2 years	77	
Rhode Island	6%–18%	1 year	5	
South Carolina	8%	1 year	46	Full %, even if early redemption
South Dakota	12%	4 years	67	
Vermont	6%–12%	1 year	14	
West Virginia	12%	1 year	55	
Wyoming	18%	4 years	23	Foreclosure required in 6 years

Total = 1,152

APPENDIX II
The 16% Winner's Circle

While this book has so far given you an overview of how to buy, collect on, and foreclose tax lien certificates, if you are ready to roll up your sleeves and try what you have learned in a particular state, you will need to study the details of that state's laws.

In this appendix, I have selected those states which pay 16% or more on their tax lien certificates. In addition, I have included a few more because they are temporarily paying only slightly below that rate, or because they illustrate some interesting variation in procedures. This appendix, then, gives you a close-up view of the winners.

For those of you who want to review the full text of the original statutes in a law library, or to track them to be sure that no changes in the law have occurred after this book was published, I have noted some citations in the margin.

Arizona

When Taxes are Delinquent

§42-381 (all references are to Arizona Revised Statutes)

One-half of the yearly property taxes is considered delinquent in Arizona if they remain unpaid after November 1 at 5:00 P.M. The other half is delinquent if not paid by May 1 at 5:00 P.M. If those days are not business days, then the deadline is the next available business day.

§42-384

Each county treasurer keeps a "back tax book" and within 10 days after the first Monday in May, delinquent properties are put in this book. Until these taxes are paid, a penalty is assessed of "sixteen per cent per year simple until paid, and a fraction of a month shall be counted as a whole month."

Advertising the Sale of Tax Lien Certificates

In Arizona, the sale of tax lien certificates is not a matter of local option. Rather:

(A) The county treasurer shall advertise and sell the tax lien for the aggregate amount of all unpaid taxes becoming delinquent on the property during each and every preceding year, together with all penalties, interest, and charges respectively due for the current or prior years.   *§42-386*

Each county treasurer will prepare a notice of auction at his offices which will contain a list of delinquent properties. He must advertise this sale in two consecutive weekly issues of the "officially designated county newspaper." The ad must run between two and three weeks before the sale. Additional notice will be posted near the door to the treasurer's office. Notice will also be given to the delinquent owner.   *§42-387*

Tax Lien Auction

The tax lien sale is held in February of each year. All liens are put up for sale. If no bid is made on a lien, the treasurer tries to sell it each following day, "until all tax liens are sold or until the county treasurer becomes satisfied that no more sales can be made . . ."   *§42-390*

The auction itself works this way:

(A) When a real property tax lien is offered for sale for delinquent taxes . . . it shall be sold to the person who pays therefore the whole amount of delinquent taxes, interest, penalties, and charges then due on the property, and who in addition offers to accept the lowest rate of interest upon the amount so paid in order to redeem the property from the sale which shall not exceed the rate of sixteen per year simple from February 1 until redeemed.   *§42-393*

(B) For the purposes of this section a fraction of the month shall be counted as a full month.

The entire amount of the bid "must be paid in cash at the time of the sale."   *§42-394*

After the sale, the tax lien certificate is issued for a $1.00 fee.   *§42-395*

Buying Unsold Tax Liens

§42-390

As for those tax liens that remain unsold in the auction process, the county treasurer "shall assign to the state the property tax liens remaining unsold . . . and issue to the state a certificate of purchase . . ."

§42-401

After the certificate is issued to the state, it does not actually go anywhere. Instead, the county treasurer will assign the tax lien certificate to a buyer such as you, who sends in the amount of the taxes, interest, penalties, and charges. A tax lien certificate bought this way will yield the full 16% maximum, without the competition of an auction.

Lost Tax Lien Certificates, Assignments

§42-399

If the certificate is lost, it can be replaced if the buyer supplies a notarized affidavit and a $5.00 fee.

§42-396(b)

The tax lien certificate "shall be assignable by endorsement, and an assignment when noted on the record of tax lien sales in the office of the county treasurer shall vest in the assignee all the right and title of the original purchaser."

Paying Subsequent Years' Taxes

§42-400

Once you have a tax lien certificate, you may decide to pay the following years' tax, when they, too, become delinquent. The advantages of this are (1) that this additional money starts earning high interest, (2) that you avoid the auction, and (3) that you solidify your position as the sole lienholder in case the property is foreclosed.

On or after June 1 of each year, any person desiring to pay subsequent taxes, accrued interest, and related fees then due upon the real property for which he or she holds a certificate of purchase shall exhibit the certificate to the county treasurer, who shall endorse thereon the amount of the subsequent taxes paid and the date of payment.

A $1.00 charge is made for this transaction.

Payment of Certificate Holder

The property owner can redeem "at any time before the expiration of three years from the date of sale, or thereafter at any time before the delivery of the treasurer's deed to the purchaser . . ."

§42-421

As soon as the property owner redeems, the county treasurer will pay the lienholder on demand the amount owed upon surrender of the tax lien certificate. If only a portion of the lien is paid (for example, by a person who owns less than the entire property) the tax lien certificate will be endorsed with the portion paid.

§42-427

Foreclosing on a Tax Lien

At any time after the expiration of three years from the sale of a tax lien, if the lien is not redeemed, the purchaser, his heirs or assigns . . . may bring an action . . . to foreclose the right to redeem.

§42-451

The foreclosure action results in a judgment "commanding the county treasurer to execute and deliver forthwith to the party in whose favor judgment is entered . . . a deed conveying the property described in the certificate of purchase. After entry of judgment the parties whose rights to redeem are thereby foreclosed shall have no further right, title or interest in the property, either in law or in equity."

§42-452

The property owner can still dash in after the foreclosure action is brought but before the judgment is issued and redeem the property, but if he waits that long, he must also pay the costs and reasonable attorney's fees of the tax lien holder who is foreclosing.

§42-454

Instead of foreclosing in court after three years, the holder of the tax lien certificate can decide to wait five years. At that time, the lienholder can simply go to the county treasurer and ". . . apply for and receive a treasurer's deed to the property." This process requires additional notice to the property owner and posting of the property, as well as paying $5.00 plus costs.

§42-461

Whatever process is used, the result is a brand new treasurer's deed to the property.

§42-464

Local Variations

Even though the basic procedures are set by state law, each county will have its own variations. The following is the explanation of the tax lien procedures published by Maricopa County, where Phoenix is located. You will notice some details not covered in the statutes summarized above.

TAX LIEN INFORMATION

AUCTION

The Tax Lien Sale provides for the payment of delinquent secured property taxes by an investor. The tax lien on the property is sold in open competitive bidding based on the least percent of interest to be received by the investor.

The investor is responsible for ALL research involved in the estimation of money due and in regards to the parcel description and the location of the property.

Once the tax on a secured property becomes delinquent, any previously uncollected taxes are added together for the Back Tax Lien Sale the following February.

Parcels whose liens are subject to sale will be advertised in a Maricopa County newspaper of general circulation. Copies of the newspaper will be available at the newsstand price in the Treasurer's Office.

PRE-SALE REQUIREMENTS

Prior to bidding, all bidders MUST provide the Treasurer's Customer Service Department with a complete Bidder Information Card. These cards may be obtained in the Customer Service Department.

BID PROCEDURE

Each bidder will be assigned a number for use during the bidding process. In offering these liens for sale, the parcel number and the amount shall be read in the order they appear in the newspaper. Vocal bids will be recognized by calling the bidder number. ALL SALES ARE FINAL!

The successful bidder will pay the whole amount of taxes, interest, fees, and charges then due within 24 hours. If at the beginning of the next day's session the payment has not been made, the parcel(s) will be reoffered.

The sale will continue until all liens are sold or the lack of bidding warrants discontinuing the sale.

BID INTEREST

Bids must be on the basis of interest income to the bidder.

1. The maximum bid is 16% interest per annum, prorated monthly. The lowest acceptable bid is 0% per annum.

2. The successful (lowest) bid will determine the rate of interest to be paid on the Certificate of Purchase lien, representing the amount of taxes, interest, fees and charges then due.

REDEMPTION OF LIENS

If the owner redeems the property, the investor receives his money back plus the rate of interest he bid at the sale.

DEEDS

When an owner fails to redeem prior to the expiration of three years from the date of sale, the investor may apply for a court ordered deed to the property. A Treasurer's Deed may be applied for after five years from the date of sale. For further information concerning the application for deeds, please contact the Tax Information Department of the Treasurer's Office.

ASSIGNMENTS

Assignments offer the investor an alternative way to purchase liens on parcels at a time other than the back tax sale.

The unsold parcels "struck off to the state" at the tax lien sale are available to lienholders by "assignments." The assignment of State CPs beings April 1 in the Treasurer's Customer Service Department.

Available parcels are listed as "STATE CP" in the printout located in the Customer Service Department. This printout lists the tax figure, as well as the year involved. The buyer will pay the entire amount of taxes, interest, fees, and charges due at the time of assignment. There is an additional $5.00 fee for each assignment.

The final date for purchasing assignments is December 31. The remaining assignments are prepared for the Back Tax Lien Sale in February.

NOTE: If a parcel also has current delinquent taxes in addition to "State CP" taxes, the investor may purchase both after June 1, and prevent the parcel from going to the lien sale in February.

ASSIGNMENT PURCHASING

The buyer will submit a list of desired parcels to the Treasurer's Office, along with a Cashier's Check, Money Order, or Certified Check for the approximate total. The submittals will be recorded and processed in the order in which they are received.

The calculations will be made on the assignments up to the amount received. The buyer will be notified as soon as possible if the funds on hand are insufficient to cover all parcels requested. Parcels not covered by funds on hand must remain available to other buyers.

Should the original payment be in excess of the amount due, a refund will be issued.

Be sure to specify "assignment" in order that a redemption is not inadvertently processed. The interest earned on the assignment will be the current statutory maximum (i.e., 16%).

SUBTAX

Subsequent Tax can be added to an existing lien to protect the CP holder's fiduciary interest. The subtaxing of the current year taxes onto existing Certificates of Purchase beginning June 1.

The CP holder is responsible for research of the subtax due. The subtax will consist of taxes, interest, and fees dependent on the date the taxes are being paid. There is an additional $1.00 fee for each Certificate of Purchase submitted for subtax to be applied for each year requested.

CP holders are eligible to subtax from June 1 to December 31. All remaining subtaxes will be prepared for the tax lien sale the following February.

To pay the subtax the CP holder must submit the current CP with a Cashier's Check, Money Order, or Certified Check.

If the payment is in excess of the amount due, a refund will be issued. If the funds on hand are insufficient to pay the subtax the CP holder will be notified as soon as possible. Parcels not covered by funds on hand must remain available to other purchasers.

The interest earned on subtax is at the same rate as that of the original Certificate of Purchase.

LOST CERTIFICATES OF PURCHASE

The CP holder must file a notarized affidavit with the Treasurer attesting to the loss of the certificate along with a $5.00 fee. The Treasurer will then issue an exact duplicate of the Certificate of Purchase.

TRANSFER OF CERTIFICATES OF PURCHASE

If not redeemed, a CP may be transferred by signature to another person who has a Bidder Information Card on file with the Treasurer's Office. There is a $5.00 transfer fee. The Treasurer's Office MUST be notified of the transfer to be VALID. The Treasurer pays the redeemed taxes to the last CP holder on record.

IMPORTANT TELEPHONE NUMBERS

CUSTOMER SERVICE . . . . (602) 506-8511

TAX INFORMATION . . . . (602) 506-8518

PROPERTY . . . . (602) 506-3532

ADMINISTRATION . . . . (602) 506-3675

ASSESSOR'S OFFICE . . . . (602) 506-3406

POST SALE NOTE: Each CP holder will receive a legal document called a Certificate of Purchase, identifying each parcel for which the CP holder has acquired the tax lien.

NOTE: Please furnish clerk with a parcel number when making any inquiry on your property. This information is located in the upper left-hand corner of your tax statement or on the top center of your Certificate of Purchase.

MARICOPA COUNTY TREASURER'S OFFICE
301 WEST JEFFERSON, ROOM 100
PHOENIX, ARIZONA 85003-2199

Phone Numbers to Get You Started

Maricopa (Phoenix)	(602) 506-8511
Pinal (Florence)	(602) 868-6425
La Paz (Parker)	(602) 669-6145
Gile (Globe)	(602) 425-3231

(Ask for the Treasurer's Office)

Colorado

Tax lien auctions in most states award the winning bid to the person willing to accept the *least rate* of interest. Colorado is more pragmatic. In Colorado, you have the winning bid if you are willing to fork over the *most cash* to the state. You cannot get too enthusiastic about this process, however, because any extra money you pay will not be returned even if the property owner redeems. This is simply another way of lowering the interest rate, except that the county, rather than the delinquent property owner, benefits from the competition.

While the statutes talk of a sale *of the properties,* in fact the buying of a "Certificate of Purchase" does not allow possession until the expiration of the redemption period.

Unlike other states, where the interest rate is fixed, the rate of interest the delinquent property owner must pay is changed each year to be 9% above the best rate a bank can get from the Federal Reserve. For example, if the discount rate is 4%, you will earn 13%. At the moment, we are holding Colorado's place in the "winner's circle" as a sentimental choice, because the effective rate there is at present only 12%. But we think it will go up.

Notification of Sale

By September 1 of each year, taxpayers are notified if their taxes are delinquent. Twenty days later, a list of delinquent properties is prepared, and a notice is sent that the property will be sold at a public auction.

Next, the sale of the properties is advertised in four weekly issues of a newspaper and posted in the office of the treasurer.

§§39-11-101, 39-11-102 (All section references are to Title 39, Colorado Revised Statutes Annotated)

Conduct of the Sale

§§39-11-108,
39-11-109

The tax sale is held on or before the second Monday in December of each year. The sale continues from day to day, except for Saturday and Sunday, until all the certificates are sold or until it is evident that they will not be sold.

§§39-11-111,
39-11-115

The certificates are sold "to the persons who pay therefor the taxes, delinquent interest and costs then due thereon or who further pay the largest amount, in cash, in excess of said taxes, delinquent interest and costs. Said excess amount in cash shall be credited to the county general fund." Just so there is no mistake about the desire for cash, the statutes repeat that the purchase price is to be paid in cash.

Each county can make its own rules about the minimum bid increase and the order of bidding.

§39-11-117

The successful bidder will get a "Certificate of Purchase," which indicates the rate of interest.

For information about the date of the sale and details about local procedures, contact the county beginning in December.

Assignment of Certificates

§39-11-118

Certificates of purchase are "assignable by endorsement." If the assignment is registered, the buyer gets "all right and title of the original purchaser."

Lost Certificates

§39-11-120

If a Certificate of Purchase is lost, upon presentation of satisfactory evidence, a new one will be issued.

Payment of Following Years' Taxes

§39-11-119

The holder of a Certificate of Purchase may present the certificate and pay delinquent taxes for the following year. The additional payment earns interest at the same rate as does the original purchase.

Redemption by Property Owner

At any time before a Treasurer's Deed is issued, as described below, the property owner can redeem the property by paying costs and interest at a rate "nine percentage points above the discount rate, which discount rate shall be the rate of interest a commercial bank pays to the federal reserve bank in Kansas City using a government bond or other eligible paper as security and shall be rounded to the nearest full percent." This rate is determined each year on September 1, and becomes effective October 1. For example, the discount rate in September 1, 1993, was 3%. The interest rate for redemptions on certificates sold in November 1993 will be 12%.

§39-12-103

If the property owner redeems, the holder of the Certificate of Purchase is paid upon surrender of the certificate.

§39-12-109

Obtaining a Treasurer's Deed

If the property owner does not redeem, three years from the date of sale, and upon presentation of the Certificate of Purchase, "the treasurer shall make out a deed."

§39-11-120

Before doing this, though, the treasurer will serve the persons in actual possession of the property as well as the persons on the tax roll by personal service or, if necessary, by registered or certified mail. This notice will be not more than five months nor less than three months before the deed is issued. In addition, notice will be published at three weekly intervals.

§39-11-128

Void Deeds and Certificates

If the Treasurer makes a mistake (for example, if the taxes were really paid, but not properly credited) the buyer will be paid interest by the county, only at 2% above the set discount rate rounded to the nearest percentage point, but no lower than 8%.

§39-12-111

The statute of limitations for the property owner to attack a Treasurer's Deed is five years after its issuance. This period can be up to nine years, however, under certain circum-

§§39-12-101,
39-12-104,
39-11-133

stances. You can bring a "quiet title" action (a lawsuit to confirm that you have good title) to cut short this possibility.

§39-12-104   Should you lose the property, you may have a claim for improvements you made to it.

Local Variations

The following is an explanation by the San Miguel county treasurer, located in Telluride, of how tax lien certificates are issued in her county:

TREASURER'S TAX LIEN SALE INFORMATION

THE SAN MIGUEL COUNTY TREASURER
(303) 728-4451
P.O. BOX 488
TELLURIDE, COLORADO 81435

PRE-SALE HAPPENINGS

- Property tax liens to be sold at sale are advertised in November.
- Advertisement is made once a week for four consecutive weeks.
- Property tax liens are *advertised* alphabetically, and sold in that order.
- Advertisement is made in general circulation newspaper in San Miguel County.
- Persons interested in investing in tax liens to be sold should contact the Treasurer's Office and ask to be placed on the investors' mailing list.
- Updated advertising lists, which record all delinquent property taxes paid before the sale, are available for inspection in the County Treasurer's Office.

TAX SALE PROCEEDINGS

- San Miguel County's tax lien sale is always scheduled in December.
- The sale is normally held on the first Friday in December.
- The sale begins at 10:00 A.M. and continues until all tax liens are offered.
- The sale is conducted in auction fashion.
- To facilitate the bidding procedure, each tax lien is initially offered in sequence, for the amount of taxes, interest, and penalties due. The tax lien is sold to the person who bids the highest amount. Premium bids are in excess of the taxes, interest, and penalties as advertised. All *premium* bids are at the investor's expense.
- The sale is conducted as rapidly as possible, consistent with the objectives of the sale and fair play to the bidders.

BIDDER'S CORNER

So you've decided to bid:

1) Please attend the sale at least one hour before it commences.
2) All bidders must complete a registration card stating their name, address, and phone number.
3) All bidders after completing the registration card will receive a bid number.
4) All successful bids must be paid immediately following the tax lien sale to the San Miguel County Treasurer's Office in cash, cashier's check, or personal check. This office re-serves the right to demand cash or a cashier's check.
5) The county treasurer and/or staff *reserves the right to refuse* any person from bidding at the tax lien sale.

GENERAL INFORMATION

Purchasing delinquent tax liens at sale is becoming an increasingly popular form of investment.

Interested? Here are some facts to help you understand what tax lien sale investment is and what it is NOT.

• When you purchase the tax lien sale certificate on property, you become a lien holder on the property.

• You purchase the tax lien, NOT the property! In San Miguel county, eventual transfer or deed has occurred in less than 1% of all purchases.

• Investing in tax liens through purchase at a tax lien sale is just that—an investment. The purchase can be thought of in terms of a potentially long-range certificate of deposit. Redemption of the certificate is always at a guaranteed rate of return, and can occur up until the time a Treasurer's Deed is issued.

• Each year the Colorado Banking Commission determines the rate of return. The annual percentage rate is set at nine points above the federal discount rate for September 1 of that year.

AFTER THE SALE . . .

Subsequent Years' Taxing

After August 1 of each year, all tax lien sale certificate holders have first option to purchase any subsequent years' taxes which remain unpaid. These tax liens may be endorsed to the original certificate at the same guaranteed rate of return.

Treasurer's Deed Application

If the original certificate is held for three years, the investor may apply for a Treasurer's Deed to the property. Deed application involves:

- Surrender of certificate.
- Remittance of $150 deposit to cover:
    advertising fees
    certified mail fees
    title search fees
    miscellaneous legal fees

Once application is made, the Treasurer's office:

- Advertises and posts public notice on the property
- Notifies anyone with a legal interest in the property

If redemption is made before deed issuance, all redemption and deposit monies will be returned to the investor.

When a Treasurer's Deed is issued, all outstanding tax lien sale certificates must be cleared by redemption through this office.

Phone Numbers to Get You Started

Denver (Denver)	(303) 640-4867
La Plata (Durango)	(303) 259-4000
Saguache (Saguache)	(303) 655-2656
San Miguel (Telluride)	(303) 728-4451

(Ask for the Treasurer's Office)

Florida

Florida pays a good rate of interest (18%), but makes it much harder than other states to get the property. Rather than just issuing a deed (as, for example, in Arizona) in Florida the property is sold at auction. You can bid in your tax lien certificate, but you are competing against anyone else who wishes to bid for the property.

Rules 12D-13.45 (all citations to Rules are to the Florida Administrative Code Rules)

Time of the Tax Lien Auction

Tax lien certificates on properties with delinquent taxes are sold on or before June 1 of each year.

Conduct of the Auction

FS §197.432 (all citations to "FS" are to the Florida Statutes)

Each county's tax collector will begin to sell the available tax certificates at the yearly auction. Certificates which are not sold will be bought by the county, which will get the maximum rate allowed, 18% per year, simple interest.

Rules 12D-13.45

The tax lien certificate is sold "to the person who will pay the tax, interests, costs, and charges and who will demand the lowest rate of interest, not in excess of 18 percent per year." The bidding, therefore, begins at 18% interest and goes down from there. The "charges" include the cost of advertising.

The bidding on interest rates is by fractions of one-quarter of 1%. Therefore, if a bidder offers 17½% interest, the next acceptable bid will be 17¼%.

As soon as you are the lowest bidder, you must give the tax collector a deposit of at least 10% of the total money due, or whatever higher percentage has been set.

When the tax lien certificate has been prepared, the tax collector will notify you, often by phone, and you must then get the remainder of the money owed to the tax collector within 48 hours. If you do not pay on time, you will lose your deposit.

Void Certificates

FS §§197.432, 197.443, Rules 12D-13.06

A tax lien certificate is occasionally void, either because the taxes on the property had really been paid, or because of some error in procedure or because of an inadequate description of the land. In such a case, your money will be refunded, plus you will receive consolation interest of 8% per year simple interest from the county.

Lost or Destroyed Certificates

FS §197.132

If a tax lien certificate is lost or destroyed, an application for a duplicate, accompanied by your affidavit, can be made to the board of county commissioners. The fee for the duplicate is $2.00.

Transfer of Certificates

A Florida tax lien certificate can be transferred by endorsement at any time before it is redeemed or until a tax deed is issued after foreclosure. Before the transfer is recognized, however, so that the transferee will be paid any proceeds, the holder of the certificate must send the certificate in, along with a request for transfer. A charge of $1.00 is made for this service.

FS §197.462
Rules 12D-13.54

Buying Certificates Not Sold at the Auction

As I noted above, any certificates not sold at the auction will belong to the county and are held by the tax collector of that county. You can buy these certificates from the county and get the automatic 18% highest rate, without bidding.

Under regulations in effect until recently, if you wanted to buy a county-owned certificate, you would have to pay not only the value of that certificate, but also taxes, interest, penalties, and charges for any other years for which taxes are unpaid. This total amount became the face value of the certificate. This required the outlay of more cash, but then you would earn 18% on this larger amount. New regulations omit the requirement that you buy all the outstanding tax liens on the property.

Florida Jur. 2d
21:284, 21:313
and Supp. 1991.

Payment of Lienholder on Redemption

A tax lien certificate can be redeemed at any time before the property is foreclosed upon and sold for the taxes. Anyone, including a mortgage holder, may pay the redemption costs.

If the property owner redeems the certificates, he must pay, in addition to the face amount of the certificate, any accrued interest, costs, and charges. One bonus is that even if the redemption is prompt, the property owner must still pay you a minimum of 5% interest to redeem your certificate.

FS §197.472

Application for a Tax Deed

*FS §§197.482,
197.502,
197.542;
Rules 12D-13.60,
12D-13.62-65*

A tax deed is a deed to a property issued by the government. It wipes out the title of the former owner, as well as the interest of his mortgage holder. In Florida, you will only receive a tax deed if you are the successful bidder at the tax sale.

Any time after two years have elapsed since April 1 of the year you were issued your tax lien certificate, you can file the certificate along with $15 and an application for a tax deed.

While you can do this after two years, you do not want to wait seven years, because if you have not yet taken action by that time, the certificate expires and becomes worthless.

When you apply for a tax deed, you must be prepared to pay in more than just your tax lien certificate. You must also pay all other taxes owing on the property, as well as the amount required to redeem all other tax certificates on the property, including interest and penalties. Finally, you will need to pay for a title search.

If the property is homesteaded, you will also have to pay one-half of the appraised value of the property.

The Tax Sale

After the application and the required charges are received, the tax collector delivers the application and his certification to the local circuit court. The tax sale is advertised for four consecutive weeks, and notice is sent to various persons, including the property owner and any holder of a mortgage on the property. The sale cannot be held until 30 days after the first publications.

The successful bidder must pay for the property within 24 hours by cash, a cashier's check, a bank draft, or a money order. If you did not buy the property, you will be paid the value of your certificate, plus the amount of your application, and additional interest of 18% per year from the time of your application, even if your certificate bore a lower rate of interest.

*Florida Jur. 2d
§§21:367,
21:376*

Issuance of the Tax Deed

The sale process ends with the issuance of a tax deed. Although, as noted above, this deed extinguishes the interest of the former owner and his mortgage holder, restrictive covenants running with the land are not extinguished. Occasionally, these can be bothersome, so it is worthwhile knowing the state of the title.

Assuming that the former owner has not vacated the property, you can apply to the circuit court for a writ of assistance to evict the former owner.

FS §197.562

Challenges to the Tax Deed

After the sale, the former owner may challenge the sale on a variety of grounds, including assertions that the procedures were not proper or that the taxes had been paid. You may bring a suit to quiet title or to foreclose in order to head off any such challenges.

Florida Jur. 2d 21:430, et seq.

If it turns out that the sale was invalid for some reason other than prior payment of taxes, the sale will be canceled, but then you must be paid 12% per year from the date of the issuance of the deed, and all legal expenses in obtaining the deed. In addition, you must be paid the fair cash value of all permanent improvements you made to the property.

FS §197.602

Should you decide to go into "actual possession" of the property, then a four-year statute of limitations is triggered for anyone challenging your title under the tax deed. You have the same four years to bring an action against anyone other than the former owner in "adverse possession" (i.e. squatting) on the land.

Florida Jur. 2d FS §§21:464-21:476

Local Procedures

As with the other states, each county has variations of procedure. The following is the announcement by Dade County, Florida (where Miami is located), for their annual sale of tax lien certificates:

FINANCE DEPARTMENT
OFFICE OF THE TAX COLLECTOR
140 WEST FLAGLER STREET
14TH FLOOR
MIAMI, FLORIDA 33130
(303) 375-5447
FAX (305) 375-4601

199_ TAX CERTIFICATE SALE OF 199_ DELINQUENT REAL PROPERTY TAXES

PLACE: 140 W. Flagler Street
9th Floor Conference Room
Miami, Florida

WHEN: The tax sale begins on June 1, 199_ at 8:30 A.M. to 4:00 P.M. and continuing each succeeding workday until all tax certificates have been offered for sale.

LUNCH: 12:00 noon to 1:00 P.M.

TAX SALE PROCEDURES

• In compliance with Internal Revenue Service and Department of Revenue directive, tax certificate buyers must complete and file form W-9, "Payer's Request for Taxpayer Identification Number and Certification" (TIN) at the Tax Collector's Office.

• *A single buyer number will be assigned for each Social Security or Employer Identification number* certified on the above form. The name provided for the buyer number and TIN *must be identical.*

• A $2000 deposit is required for each tax buyer prior to participation in the sale. This deposit will be applied to the purchase of tax sale certificates. If no tax certificates are purchased, the deposit will be returned about one month after the end of the tax sale.

- An additional deposit of at least 10% must be made each day on the amount of tax certificates purchased on the prior day. If a timely deposit is not made, continued participation in the tax sale will not be authorized until the account is settled.
- Payment will be accepted in the Tax Collector's Office; make checks payable to DADE COUNTY TAX COLLECTOR.
- Parcels are identified by item numbers and tax certificates will be sold in the order that they are advertised.
- The bidding for each parcel shall start at eighteen percent (18%) and shall be accepted in even and in fractional increments of one quarter percentage (1/4%) points only.
- Tax certificates shall be struck off to the party who demands the lowest rate of interest on the amount of tax due. *Tax certificates will be issued only in the name identified by the buyer number and TIN.*
- *Within forty-eight (48) hours from the mailing of the notice that tax certificates are ready for delivery and the amount necessary to pay, payment in full must be made in the form of certified check, bank draft, or money order.* (No cash or personal checks please.)
- After payment of balance due and execution of ownership acknowledgment, a single tax certificate summarizing all certificates purchased at the tax sale will be issued to the buyer, together with a detailed listing identifying purchases by folio, advertising sequence number, year, type, certificate number, interest rate, and certificate face amount.
- FAILURE TO MAKE PAYMENT WITHIN FORTY-

EIGHT HOURS OF THE CERTIFIED NOTICE POSTMARK SHALL CAUSE THE DEPOSITS TO BE FORFEITED, IN WHICH CASE THE BIDS SHALL BE CANCELED AND THE TAX CERTIFICATE(S) RESOLD.

- The Tax Collector or Deputy Tax Collector conducting the tax auction has full authority and responsibility to conduct the sale in accordance with the provisions of Chapter 197, Florida Statutes and Department of Revenue rules.

No scheme or procedure shall be developed by bidders that defeats the competitive nature of the tax sale.

DELINQUENT REAL PROPERTY TAXES
TAX CERTIFICATE SALE
GENERAL INFORMATION

- REAL ESTATE TAXES—in the State of Florida—are due and payable starting NOVEMBER 1st for the calendar year beginning January 1, each year.
- Discounts ranging from 4% in the month of November to 1% in the month of February are allowed for early payments. The gross tax amount is payable in March. Normally, TAXES BECOME DELINQUENT ON APRIL 1, following the year in which they were assessed.
- By law, the Tax Collector is required to conduct an annual TAX CERTIFICATE SALE on delinquent real estate properties starting on or before June 1. Delinquent real estate parcels are advertised in a local publication of general circulation (Miami Review) once each week for four weeks prior to the tax certificate sale.
- TAX CERTIFICATES ARE A FIRST LIEN on real estate and are "struck off" to the person who will pay the tax, interest, advertising cost, tax collector's commission of 5%, and will demand the

lowest rate of interest, not in excess of 18% per year.

- ANYONE MAY PARTICIPATE IN A TAX CERTIFICATE SALE, IF THEY FIRST OBTAIN A BUYER'S NUMBER AND MAKE A REASONABLE DEPOSIT IN THE AMOUNT SPECIFIED BY THE TAX COLLECTOR. A minimum deposit of 10% must be made each working day for certificate purchases of the prior day.
- Note: Taxes may be paid at any time prior to the item in the publication coming up for bidding. Therefore, many listed properties will not be sold.

!CAUTION!
TAX CERTIFICATE BUYERS ARE
NOT PURCHASING PROPERTY AT
A TAX CERTIFICATE SALE.

- If there are NO BIDDERS for the delinquent taxes, the tax certificate is struck off to the County at the maximum rate of 18%.
- NO TAX CERTIFICATES SHALL BE SOLD ON PROPERTY WHICH HAS BEEN GRANTED A HOMESTEAD EXEMPTION WITH LESS THAN $100.00 DELINQUENT TAXES.
- The Tax Collector must initiate action to cancel any improperly issued tax certificate or deed in accordance with Florida Statutes.
- All tax certificates issued to an individual MAY BE TRANSFERRED by official endorsement, witnessed by the Tax Collector, at any time before they are redeemed or a tax deed is executed. The cost is $2.00 for each certificate.
- Any person may REDEEM A TAX CERTIFICATE AT ANY TIME after it has been issued and before a tax deed is issued.
- A county-held certificate may be purchased at any time before a tax deed application has been

made, *except, no purchases or selections of county-held certificates will be accepted before completion and reconciliation of the tax sale.*

- When the interest earned on the tax certificate is less than 5% of the face amount of the certificate, a mandatory charge of five (5) percent shall be levied upon the tax certificate.
- The Tax Collector receives a fee of $5.00 for each tax certificate purchased or redeemed.
- Upon payment of delinquent taxes for which certificates have been issued, the Tax Collector will mail redemption checks and notices to the buyer of record. If requested, redemptions will be held at the Tax Collector's Office for pickup.
- Tax certificates have a LIFE OF SEVEN (7) YEARS FROM THE FIRST DAY OF THE TAX CERTIFICATE SALE.
- At any time after two (2) years have elapsed since April 1st of the year of issuance of the tax certificate, the holder may submit a TAX DEED APPLICATION to the Tax Collector of the county where the property is located. The applicant for a tax deed must pay a title search fee and all amounts required for redemption or purchase of all other outstanding tax and/or lien certificates, liens plus interest, and any omitted taxes and delinquent taxes covering the property.
- THE CLERK OF THE COURTS administers the sale of property for taxes at public auction. The tax deed is issued to the highest bidder. The opening bid on the property assessed as homestead must include all Clerk of the Courts fees and an amount equal to AT LEAST ONE HALF OF THE CURRENT ASSESSED VALUE OF THE PROPERTY.
- If the property is purchased by any person other than the certificate holder, the Clerk shall pay all sums paid by the certificate holder, plus costs and

> expenses of the application for deed with interest of 1.5% per month from the month after the date of application for deed through the month of sale.
> • For further details pertaining to all aspects of property taxes, refer to Florida Statutes 197.

Phone Numbers to Get You Started

Dade (Miami)	(305) 375-5447
Duval (Jacksonville)	(904) 630-2000
Escambia (Pensacola)	(904) 438-6500
Lee (Ft. Myers)	(813) 339-6000

(Ask for the Tax Collector's Office)

Georgia

The procedure followed in Georgia illustrates the blending of procedures between those states said to issue "tax lien certificates" and those that conduct "tax auctions," which I explained in chapter 1 ("What are Tax Lien Certificates?"). Georgia is included here because a person redeeming the property must pay a full 10% penalty for each year, or fraction of a year, following the tax sale.

This state also illustrates the wisdom of exercising the right to pay the subsequent years' taxes. In many states, the failure to pay these taxes would merely mean that there would be another holder of a tax lien certificate, and you would need to pay off that lienholder before foreclosing. In Georgia, should you fail to pay a subsequent year's taxes and also fail to promptly foreclose on the tax lien, the purchaser of a later lien may foreclose and wipe out your lien.

One of the best descriptions of state procedures was prepared by the office of Jim McDuffie, tax commissioner and ex-officio sheriff of Cobb County, Georgia, where Marietta is located. I will let Mr. McDuffie explain the process in his own words:

OFFICE OF
TAX COMMISSIONER
COBB COUNTY, GEORGIA

INTRODUCTION

There are several actions we go through in preparation for auctioning a parcel of property. We keep an information folder on these parcels that includes our title search, tax map and/or plat, copies of the newspaper advertisement, and our Ex-Officio Sheriff's Notice of Service. Our title searches are for our own purposes and would not serve the needs of the buying public. Keep in mind that it is the purchaser's responsibility to assure themselves as to the soundness of the title of all property sold at a tax sale.

Questions arise that we cannot answer, and the person interested in the property must find these answers in other offices and records. For example, we do not know building code requirements. We do not know whether county sewer lines serve any particular area or street. We have no way of knowing whether a particular parcel or lot will be approved for a building or a septic tank. We are not always aware of easements.

An important point that MUST NOT BE OVERLOOKED by the purchaser at a tax sale is that OTHER TAXES might be unpaid. If the parcel of land is located in a city that collects taxes, the city taxes could be unpaid as well. It is also possible that additional county taxes have become delinquent since proceedings were first begun on the parcel you have purchased or wish to purchase, and those additional taxes *must* be paid separately.

Can you lose money? Maybe! We don't really know. One can get a bad deed or title at a sale, whether from an individual or from a tax sale. We always recommend that anybody contemplating a tax sale consult an attorney, assure oneself the title is good, verify the information we have gathered, read those sections of Georgia law that pertain to tax sales, and attend our sales to get an idea of what goes on.

Buyers at a tax auction should find for themselves answers to questions relative to documentation, and recordation of documents resulting from the sale. The buyer is responsible for recording the Tax Deed and the Real Estate Transfer Tax form after the sale. The buyer at a tax auction is also responsible for proper processing of documents concerning the foreclosure of the owner's right to redeem and those documents concerning the right of redemption.

AUTHORITY TO SALE

The Tax Commissioner of Cobb County also serves as Ex-Officio Sheriff of Cobb County. The Tax Commissioner as Ex-Officio Sheriff appoints Ex-Officio Deputy Sheriffs, who are sworn by the Probate Judge, to act for the Tax Commissioner as Ex-Officio Sheriff in tax matters. Each Ex-Officio Deputy Sheriff has full power to advertise and bring property to sale for the purpose of collecting taxes due the state and county. (OCGA 48-5-128 and 48-2-55)

Taxes due the state and county are not only against the owner BUT are also against the property, regardless of judgments, mortgages, sales or encumbrance. Taxes constitute a general "lien" upon all property of a taxpayer and attaches on January 1st of each tax year, even though a "fifa" has not been issued. (OCGA 48-2-56 and 48-5-28)

FIFA

A FIFA (short for fieri facias)—a Latin term for "cause it to be done," and also used interchangeably with TAX EXECUTION or EXECUTION) is a tax lien or writ, authorizing the Sheriff or Ex-Officio Sheriff to obtain satisfaction of unpaid taxes by levying on and selling the delinquent taxpayer's property. These documents are recorded on the General Execution Docket "GED" of the Clerk of Superior Court. (OCGA 48-3-1 and 48-3-3)

TAX SALE PROCEDURES

The Cobb County Tax Commissioner's office follows certain procedures when it levies upon a piece of property. These procedures are prescribed by the Official Code of Georgia, Annotated (OCGA). You will see code sections referenced throughout this booklet. These references are a starting point for your research and are by no means a complete listing. We strongly suggest you read those sections of Georgia law which pertain to Tax Executions and Tax Sales. OCGA Title 48—Revenue and Taxation, Chapter 3—Tax Executions, and Chapter 4—Tax Sales, contain important information that you must be aware of. Also read and research those Opinions of the Attorney General and Judicial Decisions which are shown after each code section. These opinions and court cases are extremely important and must be taken into consideration when interpreting these laws.

On the following page, you will find a Tax Sale Flow Chart that outlines legally required procedures. We will further explain each procedure and reference code sections to which you may refer.

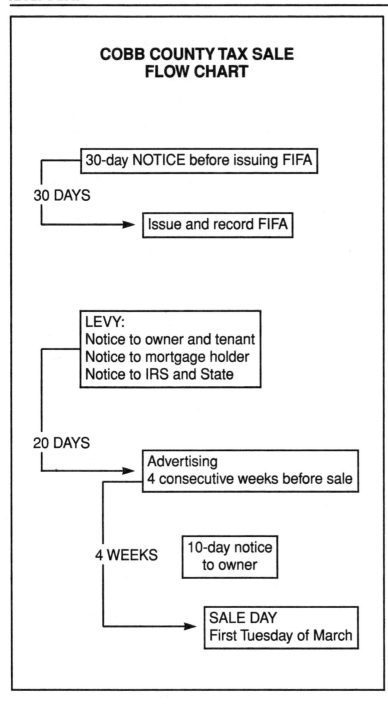

COBB COUNTY TAX SALE
FLOW CHART

30-day NOTICE before issuing FIFA

30 DAYS

Issue and record FIFA

LEVY:
Notice to owner and tenant
Notice to mortgage holder
Notice to IRS and State

20 DAYS

Advertising
4 consecutive weeks before sale

4 WEEKS

10-day notice
to owner

SALE DAY
First Tuesday of March

30-DAY NOTICE BEFORE ISSUING FIFA

As soon as the last day for payment of taxes has arrived; the Tax Commissioner shall notify, in writing, the taxpayer of the fact that the taxes have not been paid and, that unless taxes are paid within 30 days, an execution (fifa) will be issued. (OCGA 48-3-3)

ISSUANCE AND RECORDATION OF FIFA

At any time after the 30-day notice has elapsed, the Tax Commissioner shall issue executions (fifa or tax lien) against the owner and the property. The execution (fifa) is directed "to all and singular sheriffs of this state," (which means Sheriffs or Tax Commissioners who serve as Ex-Officio Sheriffs) and shall direct them to seize and sell the property of the delinquent taxpayer to satisfy the delinquent taxes. The property shall be plainly described on the execution (fifa). The execution also bears interest at the rate of 1% per month from the date the tax was due. The execution (fifa) is signed by the Tax Commissioner as Ex-Officio Sheriff or may be signed by the Sheriff in a county where the Tax Commissioner does not serve as Ex-Officio Sheriff. The execution (fifa) is then recorded on the General Execution Docket (GED) of the Clerk of Superior Court.

As far as we can tell, and according to a recent court case, *Tuggle v. IRS*, 30 Bankr. 718 (Bankr. N.D. GA 1983), prior recorded IRS liens and all State of Georgia tax liens are superior to Cobb County tax liens. (OCGA 48-2-56, 48-3-1, 48-3-3, 48-3-4, 48-3-6, 48-3-8, 48-3-21 and 48-5-161)

LEVY

Whenever any Real Estate is levied upon, the levy officer who acts as an Ex-Officio Deputy Sheriff is directed by a tax execution to seize and sell the property to satisfy the delinquent taxes. The Ex-Officio Deputy Sheriff must give 20 days written notice, before advertising, to the owner, tenant, holder of the security deed, IRS and State of Georgia (if outstanding federal tax liens or Georgia Department of Revenue liens exist). This levy notice is delivered by certified mail, and if we cannot effect service by certified (mail returned unclaimed or undeliverable), this notice is delivered to the owner and/or tenant in person. The levy shall state the owner's and/or mortgage holder's name, the tax years delinquent, the principal amount of the taxes due, the accrued cost due, and a description of the property to be sold. (OCGA 48-2-55, 48-3-1, 48-3-7, 48-3-9, 48-3-10, 48-4-3, 48-5-27, 48-5-161, 9-13-13, IRS Publication 786, and *Mennonite Board of Mission v. Adams*, 515 U.S.L.W. 4872, 77 L.Ed.2d 180 [1983])

SELECTION OF PROPERTY FOR TAX LEVY

If the property being levied upon is a house and lot, then the Tax Commissioner routinely takes it all. However, if a large parcel is being levied, it may not be prudent to sell all of it, and a portion may be set aside for levy purposes. The delinquent taxpayer may select the property to be sold. However, it is at the discretion of the Ex-Officio Deputy Sheriff to levy on additional property whenever he deems it necessary to secure prompt collection of delinquent taxes. This is known as the "pointing out privilege." (OCGA 48-3-4)

ADVERTISING

All properties to be auctioned for delinquent taxes are advertised four (4) consecutive weeks prior to the first Tuesday of the month. These advertisements are placed in the legal section of the Marietta Daily Journal under the heading "Tax Commissioner." Each advertisement shows the owner's name, a description of the property to be sold, and the amount of tax due. (OCGA 9-13-140, 9-13-141, 9-13-142, and 48-2-55)

10 DAY NOTICE TO OWNER

At least 10 days before the tax sale, the owner is sent a written notice by certified mail, informing him of the impending tax sale.

TAX SALE

On the first Tuesday of each month, between the hours of 10 A.M. and 4 P.M., we hold our tax sale on the steps of the Superior Court building (except, when the first Tuesday of the month falls on a legal holiday, the sale is held the next day, Wednesday). The opening bid for a particular piece of property is the amount of tax due, plus penalties, interest, fifa cost, levy cost, administrative levy fee, certified mail cost, and advertising cost. The property is sold to the highest bidder. If no one bids at least the amount due the county for the property, the Tax Commissioner has the authority to bid the property for the County.

PAYMENT

We require payment in full upon conclusion of the tax sale. Payment must be in the form of cash, certified check, cashier's check, or money order. We also require the purchaser to sign a statement attesting to the fact that certain property was purchased for a certain price.

Immediately following the conclusion of the tax sale, all purchasers must remit full payment to this office. After all payments are processed, we begin preparation of the Tax Deed and Real Estate Transfer Tax form. These documents are ready for pickup by Friday afternoon.

SALE CLOSING

After the tax sale, we send written notice, by certified mail, to the owner, mortgage company, IRS and the State of Georgia (if applicable) informing them the property was sold. We inform them of who purchased the property and provide them with the purchaser's address. (OCGA 9-13-160, 9-13-161, 9-13-166, 48-2-55, 48-4-1, 48-4-2, 48-4-3, 48-4-4, 48-4-5, 48-4-6 and 48-4-20)

AFTER THE TAX SALE

PAYMENT OF EXCESS FUNDS

If there are any excess funds after paying taxes, accrued cost, and all expenses of a tax sale, they shall be paid to the person "authorized to receive them". (OCGA 48-4-5)

To be "authorized to receive" these funds usually means that one has redeemed the tax deed. "In all cases where property is redeemed, the purchaser at the tax sale shall make a quit-claim deed to the defendant in FIFA, which deed shall recite: *The name of the person who has paid the redemption money.*" (OCGA 48-4-44)

After receiving the quit-claim deed and having it recorded, a copy must be presented to the Tax Commissioner. The excess funds will then be disbursed to whoever is named on the quit-claim deed as the one who redeemed the property.

Circumstances other than those described here are possible but are highly unusual. Furthermore, if any potential for conflict of claims appears, then the excess funds will be turned over to the court for a decision.

RIGHT OF REDEMPTION AND THE AMOUNT PAYABLE FOR REDEMPTION

Whenever any real property is sold at a tax sale, whether to an individual or to Cobb County, the owner, creditor, or any person having an interest in the property may redeem the property from the holder of the tax deed.

The owner, creditor, or any other person with interest in the property must pay the purchaser of the tax deed the amount paid for the property at the tax sale, plus a 10% premium of that amount for each year or fraction of a year which has elapsed since the date of sale plus costs. (A premium of 20% must be paid when Cobb County is the purchaser.)

The owner, creditor, or any other person with interest in the property may redeem the property at any time during the twelve months following the tax sale. The purchaser of the deed cannot take actual possession of the property during this time. The tax deed purchaser is not authorized to receive rents or make improvements to any structure on the property or grade any lot prior to this time.

When the property has been redeemed (all monies being due the purchaser having been paid as prescribed by law), the purchaser shall then issue a quit- claim deed to the owner of the property (as stated on the fifa) releasing the property from the tax deed.

This redemption of the property shall put the title conveyed by the tax sale back to the owner, subject to all liens that existed at the time of the tax sale. If the redemption was made by any creditor off the owner or by any person having any interest in the property, the amount expended by the creditor or the person interested shall constitute a first lien on the property. (OCGA 48-4-21, 48-4-40, 48-4-41, 48-4-42 and 48-4-43)

NOTICE OF FORECLOSURE OF RIGHT TO REDEEM

After 12 months from the date of the tax sale, the purchaser at the tax sale may terminate or foreclose on the owner's right to redeem the property by causing a notice or notices of the foreclosure to be served by certified mail to the owner of record and to all interest holders that appear on the public record. In addition, the notice of foreclosure is to be published in the county in which the property is located, once a week for four consecutive weeks in a six-month period immediately prior to the week of the redemption deadline date specified in the notice.

If redemption is not made until after the required notice has been given, then the cost of serving the notice or notices, the cost of publishing the notice and the further sum of 10% or the amount paid for the property at the sale to cover the cost of making the necessary examinations to determine the persons upon whom notice should be served, shall be added to the redemption price. (OCGA 48-4-42, 48-4-45 and 48-4-46)

AFTER THE RIGHT OF REDEMPTION IS FORECLOSED

After foreclosing the right of redemption, we recommend that the purchaser seek legal advice regarding the *petition to Quiet Title in Land*, pursuant to OCGA 23-3-60.

Under the action, the petitioner (Tax Deed Purchaser) makes a request to the court to take jurisdiction over the matter. The court then appoints a *Special Master* (third party) to examine the petition and exhibits and to determine who is entitled to notice. The petitioner will then ask the court to issue a decree establishing his/her title in the land against "all the world" and that all "clouds to petitioner's title to the land be removed" and that "said decree be recorded as provided by law."

RIPENING OF THE TAX DEED BY PRESCRIPTION

The term prescription refers to a process, whereby over a period of time, a tax deed becomes a fee simple title.

A title under a tax deed properly executed at a valid and legal sale prior to July 1, 1989, will ripen by prescription after a period of seven years from the date of execution of that deed.

A title under a tax deed executed on or after July 1, 1989, will ripen by prescription after a period of four years.

Notice of foreclosure of the right to redeem is not required in order for title to ripen by prescription.

PAYMENT OF SUBSEQUENT TAXES

Until the right of redemption has been foreclosed or the title has been ripened by prescription, a tax deed has the same force and effect of a lien. However, defeasible title has been conveyed to the tax deed purchaser and therefore liability for subsequent taxes would be the same as any superior lienholder. If there is a subsequent tax sale of the same parcel, the tax deed purchaser will be listed as the owner along with the defendant in fifa (record owner) for purposes of levy and sale, despite not having foreclosed the right of redemption or having the tax deed ripen by prescription. Therefore, not only would it be in the best interest of the tax deed purchaser to pay subsequent taxes but it could possibly enhance the tax deed purchaser's title against the record owner's title.

Even though the tax deed purchaser may receive tax bills for subsequent taxes, the owner of record will continue to be the defendant in fifa. If and when the tax deed purchaser forecloses the right to redeem or the tax deed ripens by prescription and the tax deed purchaser takes possession, the tax deed purchaser becomes the record owner.

Phone Numbers to Get You Started

Carrol (Carrolton)	(404) 830-5844
Clarke (Athens)	(706) 613-3120
Douglas (Douglasville)	(404) 920-7272
Lowndes (Valdosta)	(912) 333-5106
Cobb (Marietta)	(404) 528-8600

(Ask for the Tax Commissioner's Office)

Illinois

The process of selling tax liens is different in two respects in Illinois: First, the state has two parallel systems with different rates of interest and different procedures. The "regular system" pays a decent 18%. However, the other system, under the "Scavenger Act," pays an impressive 24% interest per year. Second, the courts are more involved in the process of selling the liens than they are in other states. For example, the tax collector must bring the lien before the court before it can be sold. This gives more assurance to a buyer that the lien will be immune from later attack. On the other hand, you are more likely to need a lawyer in this state to get you through the process.

Sale of the Liens

§§21-15, 21-115, 21-135, 21-150, 21-160 (Unless otherwise indicated, all references are to 35 Illinois Compiled Statutes 200/1-1 et seq.)

The "Regular System": After June 1 and September 1 of each year, if a property is delinquent, the tax collector will advertise a notice that he will apply for a judgment from the court allowing the sale of the property. The advertisement must be published at least 10 days before the application is made. It will list the lots, the names of the owners, the amounts due and the years for which they are due. The property owner is notified by registered or certified mail.

The judgment for sale is usually obtained in October. It will provide that on the following Monday, a sale will be held at the county building of "the properties, or so much of each of them as shall be sufficient to satisfy the amount of the taxes . . . interest, penalties, and costs."

§21-220

In order to bid at the tax lien auction, you must register 10 days before and in the larger counties you must deposit a letter of credit or bond for $1\frac{1}{2}$ times the amount of taxes and penalties due.

§21-215

The winning bid will be the one which accepts the lowest rate of interest on the tax lien to be paid by the property owner. The bidding starts at 18% and goes down from there.

Czerwionka and Kwaltzo, Illinois Tax Service §60.43[3] (1992)

Particularly in Cook County, the tax status of the property should be reviewed carefully, because other back taxes may be due which are not being sold at this auction.

The "Scavenger Act": The "Scavenger Act" applies only if a property is at least two years delinquent. Sales under this act may not occur every year in a given county, but they are supposed to take place at least once every two years. In reality, it can be longer than that between sales.

§221-145, 21-260

§221-270

In order to bid at the Scavenger Sale, you must register five business days in advance and may be required to pay a registration fee of between $50 and $100.

§221-260

Under this system, you do not bid on the amount of interest you will accept; that is fixed. Rather, you bid on the amount that you will pay for the property. As a practical matter, this may not make much difference, because if you bid an amount for the property over the amount of the delinquent taxes, and the property owner later pays off the taxes plus interest to you, the actual yield on your investment is lowered by the additional amount you bid. For example, if the amount of taxes due is $1,000, the property owner will have to pay $240 to redeem at the end of one year. If you had bid $1,100, you would only get $140 in interest.

The minimum bid on the property is $250 or one-half of the amount of taxes owed, if that is less than $500.

The successful bidder must immediately pay the minimum bid to the county collector. If your bid is for more than the minimum, you have until the next day to pay the rest. Do not neglect to pay. If you don't pay, you will forfeit your minimum bid of up to $250. As if this were not enough, a collection suit can be brought upon failure to pay.   *§§21-240, 21-260*

If you are the successful bidder, you will get a Certificate of Purchase. Before you get it, however, you must certify that you are not the delinquent taxpayer, and that you have not failed twice to complete a tax lien purchase.   *§§21-250, 21-265*

The certificate you receive is assignable by endorsement.

Redemption or Foreclosure

As in other states, the property owner can redeem the property by paying the amount of the back taxes, plus interest, penalties, and costs. If the lien was sold at the regular sale, the penalty you bid will increase by the same amount every six months. If the property was sold under the Scavenger Act, the interest you are paid will be according to the following table: *§§21-75, 21-260, 21-355*

Time since the Sale	Amount of Interest Due
less than 2 months	3%/month or part thereof
2–6 months	12%
6–12 months	24%
12–18 months	36%
18–24 months	48%
after 24 months	48% + 6%/year

§21-350   The amount of time you must wait before foreclosing varies with the type of property. The usual period is two years. For residential property under six units, however, the redemption period is two-and-a-half years. For seven or more units, the period is six months from the date of the sale if the taxes were overdue by two years. An abandoned property may be foreclosed earlier on petition.

§22-5, 22-15,   Within five months after the tax lien sale, you must give
22-30, 22-85   notice to the property owner of the sale. Within three to five months of the end of the redemption period, you must give notice of the coming expiration of the period. Then, unless you get an extension, you must petition for a deed and record it within five months of the expiration period. If you fail to do this, your certificate is void.

§21-290, 22-70   The property you get will be free of liens and encumbrances, but easements will remain. Therefore, you get the property free of a mortgage, but if the electric company has an easement for its line, you are still stuck with that.

Phone Numbers to Get You Started

Adams (Quincy)	(217) 223-6300
Kankakee (Kankakee)	(815) 937-2960
La Salle (Ottawa)	(815) 434-8217
Macon (Decatur)	(217) 427-2284
Tazewill (Pekin)	(309) 477-2284

(Ask for the Treasurer's Office)

Indiana

§§24-1, 6-1.1-24-   Indiana has a complex procedure, featuring fatal deadlines
1.5 (All references   for notices at the end of the redemption period and the bring-
are to Chapter   ing of the required court action to get a deed. Should you get
6-1.1, Burns   through this mine field, though, up to 25% interest awaits you!
Indiana Statutes
Annotated)

The Tax Lien Sale

After taxes are delinquent for 15 months, the county treasurer (or, in Marion County, where Indianapolis is located, the

Metropolitan Development Commission) notifies the county auditor, who maintains a list of the delinquent properties.

The county auditor will notify the owners of the time and place of the public auction. In Marion County, occupied residences are exempt from this auction. Notice of the sale is sent to requesting mortgage holders and displayed in a "public place of posting" for 21 days. The notice is also published once a week for three weeks.　　*§§24-2, 24-2.2, 24-3, 24-4, 24-4.1*

Not later than 10 days before the advertised day of sale, a court will examine the list of properties, and not later than five days before the sale, the court will enter a judgment and the clerk will prepare and enter an order for the sale.　　*§22-4.7*

The sale takes place on or after August 1 and before November 1 of each year. It continues until all properties have been offered.　　*§24-2*

The winning bidder must "immediately pay." Failure to pay results in a penalty of 25% of the amount of the bid. The county prosecuting attorney may sue to collect this money.　　*§§24-7, 24-8*

If the bid was for more than the taxes due, the excess goes to a "tax sale surplus fund." If the property is redeemed, the tax lien buyer will get this excess back. If the property is not redeemed, this excess goes to the delinquent taxpayer if a verified claim is filed within five years.　　*§24-7*

Immediately after receiving payment, the county auditor issues a "certificate of sale" which indicates the amount paid and the date when the purchaser is entitled to request a deed.　　*§24-9*

Assignment of the Certificate

The certificate is assignable, but the assignment is invalid unless it is endorsed on the certificate and registered with the county auditor.　　*§24-9*

Lost Certificates

A lost certificate can be replaced, but the court must issue a finding that the certificate did exist.　　*§25-4*

Pre-Redemption Notification by Buyer

Indiana's major innovation is a short redemption period, coupled with complex notification procedures. If you buy a tax lien certificate in St. Joseph County (South Bend) and Marion County (Indianapolis), the county auditor will take care of the most technical requirements. Because of the detailed and complex nature of these notices, and the extreme consequences of failing to give them exactly right, outside of these counties you should consult an attorney. At the least, these notices should be prepared with careful attention to notification dates. The summary here is only general as to the timing and content of the notices.

§§25-4, 25-4.5, 25-7

The redemption period is one year. Not less than three months nor more than five months before the expiration of this period, the tax lien buyer must give notice of the sale, the redemption period expiration date, the date on which the tax lien buyer intends to petition for a deed, and the amount required to redeem. The notice must be sent by certified mail to any person with a "substantial property interest of public record." If the address of a person with an interest in the property is unknown, notice must be given by publication for three weeks. If this notice is not given, then the lien terminates 30 days after the expiration of the redemption period. Another notice must be given of the intent to seek a court order for the issuance of the deed.

Redemption of the Property

§25-2

The percentage interest that a property owner must pay in order to redeem the property depends upon how long after the sale of the tax lien certificate the redemption occurs.

If the redemption occurs in less than six months, the interest is 10%. If it occurs in more than six months and less than a year, the interest rate is 15%. If it occurs in over a year, the interest is 25%. Special assessments and taxes for subsequent years bear 12% interest. No interest is paid on the amount in the surplus fund.

Obtaining a Tax Deed

To get a tax deed, the tax lien buyer needs to give the required notice and file a verified petition in the same court that authorized the sale. If the deed is not issued within four years, the lien terminates.

§§25-4.6, 25-7

After obtaining a tax deed, a quiet title action can be brought to determine its validity.

§25-14

Phone Numbers to Get You Started

Delaware (Muncie)	(317) 747-7717
LaPorte (LaPorte)	(219) 326-6808
Marion (Indianapolis)	(317) 327-3001
Monroe (Bloomington)	(812) 333-3510
Tippecanoe (Lafayette)	(317) 423-9207

(Ask for the County Auditor)

Iowa

In an effort to boost the sale of its tax lien certificates, Iowa dramatically increased the rate of interest its certificates pay to 24% per year. This had the desired effect, as county treasurers throughout Iowa are reporting greatly increased investor activity. In addition to high interest, the ability to foreclose on a property in a short 21 months also makes Iowa an attractive state to consider.

On the negative side, according to county treasurers, delinquent taxpayers have been hastening to pay off these liens to cut short that 24% interest. Thus, as high as Iowa's rate is, the ability to hold an 18% return in Florida, for example, might be more attractive than forever churning to maintain a 24% return. Further, competition for Iowa liens has made its auctions more competitive. Iowa is not a state, moreover, where you can buy tax lien certificates by phone and fax, directly from the county treasurers. Rather, Iowa allows purchases only at its tax lien auctions.

Finally, Iowa requires that the foreclosure occur before the end of three years.

Still, 24% is mighty impressive, and the possibilities in Iowa command attention.

When Taxes Are Delinquent

§§445.37 and 445.39 (All references are to Title 24 of the Iowa Code Annotated.)

Property tax payments are delinquent on October 1 and April 1, respectively. During this delinquency period, the property owner will owe interest of 1½% per month.

Notice of Delinquency and Sale

§446.9

Before May 1, the county treasurer will serve on the delinquent property owner by first class mail a notice containing the property description, the amount of taxes, interest, fees and costs owed, and a statement of the period allowed for redemption. This notice is published once in an official newspaper at least one week, but not more than three weeks, before the sale.

In addition to the notice to the property owner, the mortgage holder and others with interests in the property are notified.

§446.11

If for some reason service cannot be made, notice can instead be posted in the treasurer's office for two weeks.

The Sale

§446.7

The tax lien sale occurs annually, on the third Monday in June. At that time "the county treasurer shall offer at public sale all parcels on which taxes are delinquent. The sale shall be for the total amount of taxes, interest, fees, and costs due."

§446.16

The competition works like this: "The person who offers to pay the total amount due . . . for the smallest percentage of the parcel is the purchaser, and . . . the percentage thus designated shall give the person an undivided interest . . ." In other words, if the property is foreclosed, and the purchaser agreed to take less than a 100% interest in the property, he becomes a co-owner with the delinquent taxpayer.

Unlike states such as Florida and Arizona, where the competition is about interest rates, and unlike states such as Colorado, where the competition is about the amount which will be paid, in Iowa the amount to be paid and the interest rate to be earned are never in issue. In this respect, the system in Iowa resembles that in Michigan.

On the same day that the county treasurer sells tax liens on recently delinquent properties, liens that were not previously bought at other sales will also be sold. §446.18

The sale continues from day to day as long as there are bidders or until all of the available liens have been offered for sale. §446.17

The successful bidder is required to "immediately pay to the county treasurer the total amount bid. Upon failure to do so the parcel is again offered as if no sale had been made." §446.23

If there are still unsold parcels, the county treasurer can adjourn the sale for up to two months and try again. The notice of the new date will be posted in the treasurer's office. If these liens are still unsold, the sale can be adjourned repeatedly until they are sold. §446.25

The buyer will get a certificate of purchase which describes the parcel and the amount due and which certifies payment. §446.29

Lost Certificates

Should a certificate be lost, it can be replaced upon submission of an affidavit and payment of a small fee. §446.30

Assignment of Certificate

As in all other states, Iowa tax lien certificates are transferable "by endorsement and entry in the county system in the office of the county treasurer." §446.31

Redemption of the Property

The property owner can redeem by paying the county treasurer "the amount for which the parcel was sold . . . and interest of two per cent per month, counting each fraction of a month as an entire month." §447.1

§447.5   If the property owner redeems, the county treasurer issues a certificate of redemption.

Foreclosure of Lien

§447.9   One year and nine months after the sale (or nine months, if a lien over one year old was bought at the sale) the purchaser may serve the property owner and any person in possession of the property with a notice containing a description of the property, the date of the sale, the name of the purchaser, "and that the right of redemption will expire and a deed for the parcel be made unless redemption is made within ninety days from the completed service of the notice."

The purchaser must also notify the mortgage holder, any lessor or seller under a contract of sale, and those with recorded interests. The city where the property is located must also be notified. Only persons entitled to this notice are allowed to redeem the property. The costs of the notice, and the record search necessary to give it, are added to the amount required to redeem.

§446.13   Once this service is made, an affidavit stating that the service was made and stating the amount of costs required to
§446.10   make it, is filed with the county treasurer. It is this filing which completes the service.

§448.1   Immediately after the expiration of the 90 day period from completed service, the purchaser may return the certificate along with a $25 fee, and the county treasurer will issue a deed.

§448.1   Even after the recordation of the deed, restrictive covenants governing the use of the property will still be valid.

Loss of the Lien Through Failure to Foreclose

§446.37   "After three years have elapsed from the time of any tax sale, and action has not been completed during the time which qualifies the holder of a certificate to obtain a deed, the county treasurer shall cancel the sale from the county system."

Problems With the Sale

Should it turn out that the property owner owed no taxes at all at the time of the sale, the treasurer's deed is invalid. If this or other problems are the result of the county's mistake, the county will indemnify the purchaser.

§§445.61, 448.6, 448.10

The statute of limitations for raising problems with the sale is three years. However, in the case of a minor, a mentally ill person, or a prisoner, the statute of limitations expires three years after the disability is removed. Indeed, in the case of minors and "persons of unsound mind," the period of redemption is not up until one year after the disability is removed.

§§447.7, 448.12

The statute of limitations may be shortened by filing an affidavit that the deed was recorded. Those with a claim on the property will then have just 120 days to assert their interest in the parcel.

§448.15

Local Procedures

The following is from information issued by the Treasurer of Polk County (where Des Moines is located) for tax lien certificates issued after April 1, 1992 (the date when Iowa's major upgrade of its statutes went into effect).

Mary Maloney
Treasurer of Polk County

111 Court Avenue
Des Moines, Iowa 50309-2298
(515) 286-3060

NOTICE TO TAX SALE PURCHASERS OF THE TERMS AND CONDITIONS GOVERNING THE TAX SALE

The annual tax sale is held by the Polk County Treasurer on the third Monday in June at 8:00 A.M. for as long as purchasers are present. The annual sale is then adjourned to 10:00 A.M. on the third Monday of every month. If the third Monday falls on a legal holiday observed by the county, the sale for that month will be held on the fourth Monday.

The following information is provided to assist you in purchasing delinquent taxes at the tax sale:

1. All prospective bidders must register prior to the tax sale in the Tax Division of the Treasurer's Office. You may, through written notice to the Treasurer, designate an appointee to bid for you in your absence. You may also submit a written bid if you cannot attend; however, if other bids on the same parcel are received the tax lien certificate will be issued to the bidder who is present.

When more than one person offers to pay the total amount due, the person who designates the smallest percentage of the parcel for the total amount due will obtain the tax lien certificate. For example: Party "A" bids the total amount due for a 100 percent interest in the parcel. Party "B" bids the total amount due for a 90 percent interest in the parcel, etc. The percentage designated gives the tax lien certificate holder, upon the issuance of a treasurer's deed, an undivided interest in the parcel with the owner(s) of record. Bids for less than 1 percent will not be accepted.

You or the party which you represent may not be entitled to bid at the tax sale and become a tax sale purchaser by reason of having a vested interest in the parcel.

2. Parcels with delinquent taxes are offered for sale by legal description in numerical sequence by district and parcel number. It is imperative that you be prepared for the sale. You need to know the parcel(s) within each district and the corresponding legal description(s) upon which you intend to bid. The Tax Division of the Treasurer's Office can help you obtain this information in the days prior to the sale.

3. Payment is required at the time of purchase or at the conclusion of the sale. The amount collected will include all delinquent taxes, special assessments, interest, special assessment collection fees, publishing costs, and a $10.00 certificate fee for each certificate issued to you.

Payment must be in the form of a personal check, money order, any form of guaranteed funds, or cash. Two-party checks will not be accepted for payment.

4. Please allow 7 to 10 days to receive your certificate(s). This allows the Treasurer's staff time to complete posting of records, editing of certificates, and balancing the proceeds received from the tax sale.

5. A W-9 form must be completed and signed at the time of purchase, unless a form is already on file. This information is needed so that we can issue an accurate 1099-INT form with the appropriate Social Security number or taxpayer identification number.

At the end of the calendar year the Treasurer will issue a 1099-INT form to you and the Internal Revenue Service if the accumulative interest paid to you during the calendar year is equal to or exceeds $600.00. You will use this information when filing your Federal and State Income Tax Returns.

6. The tax sale certificate of purchase does not convey title to the purchaser. The title holder of record or other interested party retains the right to redeem within a specified period of time, depending on the type of tax sale. If the sale remains unredeemed after this period has expired, the purchaser may begin proceedings to obtain a Tax Deed to the parcel.

REGULAR TAX SALE

For parcels sold on or after April 1, 1992, the 90 day Notice of Right of Redemption may be issued after one year and nine months from the date of sale.

PUBLIC BIDDER SALE

The 90 day Notice of Right of Redemption may be issued nine months from the date of sale.

FAILURE TO OBTAIN DEED— CANCELLATION OF SALE CERTIFICATES ISSUED ON OR AFTER APRIL 1, 1992

After three years have elapsed from the time of the sale, if action has not been completed which qualifies the holder of the certificate to obtain a deed, the treasurer will cancel the tax sale.

7. A tax sale purchaser may pay subsequent taxes and special assessments on the same parcel on which s/he holds the tax sale certificate. The purchaser must request statements and inform the Tax Division of the subsequent payment so it is paid and recorded properly as an addition to the sale. Only items due in the current fiscal year or prior may be paid on a "sub-list." Special assessments due in future years cannot be paid until the fiscal year in which they become due. Failure to report the sublist payments will result in their omission from the redemption calculation.

Recorded sublist payments bear the same interest rate (2% per month) as the original tax sale.

8. A redeemed tax sale will include the following:

    a. The original tax sale amount, including the $10.00 certificate fee paid by the purchaser at the time of sale.

    b. Interest in the amount of 2% per month

calculated against the original tax sale amount. Each fraction of a month is counted as a whole month.

c. Subsequent tax payments paid by the purchaser and added to the amount of the sale, with interest in the amount of 2% per month. Each fraction of a month is counted as a whole month.

d. Valid costs incurred and recorded on the Tax Sale Register for action taken toward obtaining a Tax Deed. Costs not filed with the treasurer before redemption shall not be collected by the treasurer and may be recovered through a court action against the parcel owner by the certificate holder.

e. A $10.00 redemption certificate fee to be retained by the county.

9. The purchaser is responsible for checking parcels on which s/he holds the certificate of purchase for redemption. You may telephone the accounting division at 286-3035 to inquire if redemption funds are available for payment to you. **Because written notice of redemption is not provided the certificate holders, we recommend that you call on a regular basis to determine if funds are available for payment to you.**

Upon surrender of the tax sale certificate of a redeemed parcel, the Treasurer's Accounting Division will issue a check for the redemption amount, less the amount collected for the redemption certificate fee. The earliest a reimbursement could occur would be on the first business day following the cashier-validated date of redemption, as shown on the county system. The purchaser will receive a check and a copy of the redemption certificate, with a breakdown of the total amount of the redemption, to be retained for income tax purposes. The purchaser must sign the tax sale register indicating reimbursement of the redemption was received. As an alternative after redemption, you may forward the certificate to our Accounting Division and we will return payment through the mail.

If the original Certificate of Purchase has been lost or destroyed, a duplicate can be obtained from the Tax Division at a cost of $10.00.

In the event you have been reimbursed for a redemption and the taxpayer's check does not clear the taxpayer's bank account for any reason, you will be required to return the funds to the Treasurer's Accounting Division upon notification. We will return the tax sale certificate to you and cancel the redemption. The tax sale will be reinstated as of the original sale date with any subsequent redemption calculated according to the law in effect at the time of the sale.

10. The tax sale certificate of purchase is assignable by endorsement of the certificate and entry in the treasurer's register of tax sales. Please contact this office for further information should you desire to assign a certificate.

11. For each parcel sold, the treasurer is required to notify the titleholder of record that the parcel was sold at a tax sale.

12. The fee for issuance of a Treasurer's Tax Sale Deed is $25.00 per parcel.

This document has been prepared to provide general information and guidelines relative to tax sales and tax sale redemptions. It is not an all-inclusive listing of statutory requirements, procedures or policy, nor is it to be construed as a legal opinion of the statutes governing tax sales.

To protect your legal interest as a tax sale buyer and to determine your legal rights and remedies, we recommend that you consult with your legal counsel.

You may call our Tax Division at (515) 286-3871 to obtain additional information.

Effective from: April 1, 1992

Lee U. Duin
Assistant Director
Polk County Treasurer

Phone Numbers to Get You Started

Blackhawk (Waterloo)	(319) 291-2409
Dubuque (Dubuque)	(319) 589-4436
Johnson (Iowa City)	(319) 356-6087
Lynn (Cedar Rapids)	(319) 398-3466
Polk (Des Moines)	(515) 286-3060

(Ask for the Treasurer's Office)

Louisiana

Louisiana, which is a "loner" in several areas of law, has two unusual features in its tax lien certificates: first, the buyer can ask a court for immediate possession of the property. Second, the buyer will collect at least 5% in penalties no matter how soon the property is redeemed. Along with the underlying interest rate of 12%, tax liens in Louisiana pay a total of 17% for the first year.

Notification and Sale

The tax collector will notify property owners of delinquent taxes on January 2 of each year. If notification cannot be made that way, notification will be published. Notification will also be given to mortgage holders. The sale will be advertised 20 days after this notice is completed.

§§2180, 2180.1, 2181 (References, unless otherwise indicated, are to Title 47, Louisiana Revised Statutes.)

§§2181, 2181.1,
2182

The sale must be held before May 1, if possible. It is conducted any time between the hours of 8:00 A.M. and 8:00 P.M. The purchaser must pay in "cash, in legal tender money of the United States."

§2180

Within 30 days after the sale, the tax collector notifies the owner of the property of the amount required to redeem and the period allowed for redemption.

Redemption of the Property

§2183

The property owner can redeem until three years after the sale has been recorded.

§§2183; LA Constitution, Art VII §25 (1974); Canova c. State, 451 So.2d 1291, 1292, writ den. 458 So.2d 124 (1984)

The cost of redemption is set by the Louisiana Constitution, making it difficult to change in future years. That cost is a flat 5% penalty, no matter when the property is redeemed, plus 1% interest per month. While the penalty portion of the return is a great advantage if redemption occurs early during the first year, it also means that the interest rate is only 12% during the second and third years.

Still, in Louisiana the property owner will not likely wait for the second and third years, because the buyer can go into court

§2185

and get an order for immediate possession of the property!

§§2181, 2222

If the property is redeemed, the purchaser must not only be paid the principal, interest, and penalty, but also the value of all improvements made to the property. In addition, the purchaser also gets the cost of maintenance, repair, and demolition required to meet property standards ordinances.

§2183

If the property is not redeemed this "shall operate as a cancellation of all conventional and judicial mortgages."

§2228

Three years after recording the sale, the purchaser can bring a quiet title action to eliminate any contest as to the validity of the sale.

Phone Numbers to Get You Started

Bossier Parish (Benton)	(318) 965-3400
Calcasien Parish (Lake Charles)	(318) 491-3680
Lafourch Parish (Thibodaux)	(504) 448-2111
Livingston Parish (Livingston)	(504) 686-2241

(Ask for the Sheriff/Tax Collector)

Maryland

This state has high interest rates and short periods of redemption. The latter feature biases the process toward those looking toward acquiring the property, and tends to bid up the price at the sale.

Maryland is also unique in that the state is extremely indulgent of local variations, even in simple procedural matters. You should therefore be especially aware of local practices.

Notifications of Delinquent Property

The various counties in Maryland have their own rules about how delinquent a property must be before it can be sold.

Notification of sale is made by mail 30 days in advance, by posting the property (in Baltimore) and by publication in a newspaper (the number of times varying by county).

§§14-808, 14-812, 14-813 (All citiations are to the Annotated Code of Maryland.)

Conduct of the Auction

The property is sold at auction for at least the amount of taxes, interest, penalties and expenses. "[T]he lien for the taxes, interest, penalties and expenses passes to the purchaser." In Baltimore, a vacant and abandoned building can be sold for less than this amount.

§14-817

No later than the day after the sale, the successful bidder must pay to the tax collector at least the taxes due. The rest of the purchase price need not be paid until "[a]fter the final decree has been passed foreclosing the right to redemption . . ."

Soon after the sale, a "Tax Sale Certificate" will be issued.

§14-820

Rates of Interest

The rate of interest paid if the property is redeemed varies by county. Assuming that the county did not decide differently, for example, the rates would be 14% in Carroll County and 10% in Caroline County. The rate in Baltimore is presently 24%.

§14-820

Unless the tax collector has received written notice of an

§14-827

assignment giving the name and address of the assignee, he is authorized to treat the original purchaser as the holder of the certificate of sale and to pay any redemption money to him.

Required Foreclosure

§14-833

After six months from the date of sale, you may sue to foreclose on the certificate of sale. The property owner can redeem until the decree is filed.

Foreclosure is *required* within two years in this state. However, if you bought a lien on a building in Baltimore which is vacant and abandoned or which got a building violation notice (whatever you do, do *not* do that) you must foreclose within one year.

The judgment of foreclosure cannot be reopened, except for fraud, after one year.

Phone Numbers to Get You Started

Allegheny (Cumberland)	(301) 777-5965
Cecil (Elkton)	(410) 996-5385
Charles (La Plata)	(301) 645-0685
St. Mary's (Leonardtown)	(301) 475-4472

(Ask for the Treasurer's Office in Cecil, Charles and St. Mary's Counties. Ask for the Tax and Utilities Office in Allegheny County. Ask for the Tax Collector's Office in the City of Baltimore.)

Massachusetts

§29 (All references are to Chapter 60, Annotated Laws of Massachusetts.)

Massachusetts is serious about collecting its taxes. An old law, obviously not enforced, reserves the right to throw a property owner in jail if he even *looks* like he might not pay, even if the tax isn't due yet:

> If the assessors are of the opinion that the credit of a person taxed is doubtful or that he is about to leave the commonwealth, they may by special warrant direct the collec-

tor forthwith, without demand or notice, to compel payment by distress or imprisonment, whether the tax is payable immediately or at a future day, by installments or otherwise.

By comparison to these choices, a tax lien sale may appear positively festive. Indeed, the owner might decide not to object to imprisonment, if the alternative is collection "by distress." (Actually, "distress" means seizing the property to compel payment.) Massachusetts gives its tax collectors several ways to collect taxes, and tax lien sales are rare. We could find them only in Pittsfield. Check with the individual local government.

The Tax Collector's Auction

Property taxes are made a lien on property on January 1 in the year of assessment. If they are not paid within 14 days of a notice to pay, the property can then be advertised for sale.

§§1, 37, 40, 42

A notice of the time and place of the sale is published at least 14 days before in a newspaper in the town (or in a newspaper in the county, if there is no town newspaper). The notice will state the amount owed and the names of all owners and heirs. In addition, the notice will be posted "in two or more convenient public places."

At the sale, the property will be sold:

... for the amount of the taxes and interest, if any, and necessary intervening charges, for the smallest undivided part of the land which will bring said amount, or the whole for said amount, if no person offers to take an undivided part. . . .

§§43, 44

In other words, like Michigan and Iowa, the price and the interest rate are constant; the bidding is for what percentage ownership the bidders will accept upon foreclosure.

The winning bidder must immediately deposit the amount which the tax collector "considers necessary to insure good faith in payment of the purchase money . . ." If this amount is not deposited immediately, the sale is void.

§49   If the entire amount of the bid is not paid within 20 days, the sale is likewise void and the deposit if forfeited.

§45   The winning bidder gets a "collector's deed." This deed does not grant possession of the property, but it is held as security for repayment until the right of redemption expires. The deed comes with a warranty that the sale was conducted according to law.

§45   If there is no bidder at the auction, the treasurer of the city or town can sell the property at another auction.

Recording the Deed

§52   The winning bidder must be sure to record the deed promptly. The deed is invalid if not recorded within 60 days after the sale.

Appointment of Local Representative

§47   In an odd gambit, apparently to increase local employment, if the winning bidder does not reside in the town, he "shall appoint an agent residing therein . . . authorized to release such land." A resident can simply file with the treasurer and record a notice of his residential and business addresses.

Redemption of the Property

§§62, 63   The property owner can redeem by paying the amount of the lien, plus 16% per year interest and any charges which have attached.

     The money may be paid to the purchaser, or to the purchaser's designated representative or assign, or to the treasurer. This procedure is unique to Massachusetts. In other states, no option is given to pay the lienholder directly; the money always goes to the local agency.

     If the property owner pays the treasurer, but pays too little, the purchaser must demand the rest, and then sue the property owner within three months.

     The property owner need not pay the entire amount at once, however. Instead, he can pay in "installments . . . each of which, except the last, shall be in amount of not less than 25% of the total." Should the property owner elect this installment route, an extra year is given to pay the taxes without danger of foreclosure.

Foreclosure of the Property

If the tax lien purchaser is not repaid within six months, a petition can be brought in the "land court" to foreclose on the property.   *§64*

The court will notify interested persons, including mortgage holders, of a hearing date at least 20 days after the notice. On or before that date, an interested person can offer to redeem "upon such terms as may be fixed by the court." At this state, a person redeeming is also liable for attorney's fees. A person contesting the foreclosure can demand a jury trial.   *§§66, 67, 68, 71*

If no appearance is made by a person offering to redeem or contesting the proceeding, the purchaser can make a motion for a default decree. This will "forever bar all rights of redemption" except that within one year (or within 90 days if the property is abandoned) the court can vacate the decree if the property has not been resold to an innocent purchaser.   *§69*

If the tax sale is declared to be invalid, the treasurer will refund the amount paid plus interest at 6% for up to two years.   *§84A*

A state official warned that although foreclosure action can be filed in six months, between backlogged courts and property owners requesting extensions, the matter may not be completed for up to three years.

Phone Number to Get You Started

Pittsfield   (413) 499-9431

(Ask for Dave Polcaro, Jr., Tax Collector)

Michigan

Michigan is known for a whopping 50% interest rate on tax lien certificates paid in the second year of delinquency, no matter how soon the owner redeems the property. This is certainly extraordinary. As in Iowa and Massachusetts, the auction does not bid down the interest rate—it bids down the percentage ownership of the property which the successful bidder will accept. In other words, if you bid in less than 100%, and eventually get the property, you will become the owner of an undivided part interest along with the delinquent owner. You will probably have to petition a court to sell the property should you acquire a new partner in this manner.

Time of the Tax Lien Auction

Section 211.71 (All references are to the Michigan Compiled Laws.)

On the first Tuesday in May, at the office of the County Treasurer in each county, beginning at 10:00 A.M., tax lien certificates for properties delinquent in the third year after assessment are offered for sale. For example, in May 1995, the taxes from 1992 will be offered for sale.

Advertising of Available Properties

The properties for which tax liens are offered are advertised in a newspaper in each county. Michigan's Department of Treasury advises that a list of newspapers for all 83 counties is available by writing to the Department of Treasury, Local Property Services Division, Treasury Building, Lansing, Michigan 48992.

Conduct of the Auction

Each tax lien will be sold at the auction to the person who will pay the accumulated taxes and charges and *take the least undivided interest in the property.* This means that if the property goes to foreclosure, you will become a "tenant in common" with the delinquent owner to the extent of the undivided interest you bid.

Therefore, at this auction the bidding starts at 100% of the property interest. Someone willing to take only 99% of the property interest upon foreclosure has a higher bid, and so on.

Buying Unsold Tax Liens

If a tax lien is not sold at the auction, it may be bought at the Michigan Department of Treasury, Local Property Division, in Lansing. The last day that delinquent tax liens can be bought there is April 19 of the year following the sale. For example, if the tax sale is held in May 1995, unsold tax liens can be bought from the state until April 19, 1996.

The price of a certificate bought from the state must include 1¼% interest per month (15% per year).

Redemption by the Property Owner During the First Year

The property owner has the right to redeem the tax lien after the sale by paying the amount of the bid, plus 1¼% per month (15% per year), up to the time that you obtain or are entitled to obtain a tax deed, i.e., the following May. If the property owner pays the taxes, then the state treasurer will notify you to send in the certificate and claim the amount which the property owner paid to redeem. The state treasurer will take at least six weeks, sometimes longer, to process the redemption and your payment. During this time, you get no interest.

Obtaining a Tax Deed

If the property owner does not pay the taxes before the next annual tax sale, you can surrender your tax lien certificate to the state treasurer's office and get a tax deed. You should not sit on this right too long, nor should you neglect to follow the procedure for obtaining final title described below, because unless you take these actions, your tax deed expires in five years from the day you were entitled to it.

In order to get a tax deed, you need to send the original copy of your tax lien certificate to the Local Property Services *Sections 211.140, 211.141*

Division of the Department of Treasury with the required fees. That division will do a title search, and then serve notice through the sheriff upon all owners and occupants of the property. The sheriff will send you a notice of service, which you will file with the county treasurer. You must then wait six months. During that period of time, you must purchase any additional taxes which become delinquent.

After the six months, if the property owner has not redeemed, the property is entirely yours (if your bid was for 100% of the title) or else you have a new partner. To get any money out of this situation, you would probably have to petition a court to sell the property.

Redemption by the Property Owner After the First Year

Section 211.74

Up until the time of the next tax sale (i.e., the first Tuesday in May of the following year) the property owner can still redeem. This redemption right will last until a tax deed is issued and the six month redemption period triggered by this issuance has expired.

Section 211.141

In order to redeem during this next year of delinquency, however, the property owner must pay you the purchase price for the tax lien certificate, plus the $5.00 which you paid the sheriff for personal service of the notice of the tax deed, *plus 50% interest.* The 50% applies *regardless of how little time has passed,* so you should hope for an early redemption. If the property owner does redeem, you must execute a quitclaim deed (a deed in which you renounce any interest you may have in the property) in order to get your money.

Michigan's Summary of Procedures

The State of Michigan has prepared a chart of its procedures beginning with the time of eligibility for the tax deed:

WHO	**DOES WHAT**
Tax Title Buyer	1. Surrenders original copy of purchase certificate to Local Property Services Division.
Local Property Services Division	2. Prepares tax deed and forwards to tax buyer.

NOTE 1: A tax deed cannot be issued until 1 year following the annual tax sale.

NOTE 2: A tax deed is valid for only 5 years from the date it can first be issued.

EXAMPLE: The delinquent 1986 taxes were sold at the 1989 tax sale. The tax title buyer became eligible for a tax deed on May 1, 1990. The tax deed will become void on the first Tuesday in May 1995 if the tax title buyer fails to take action.

3. Determines the following:

a. The last grantee(s) in the regular chain of title to the land or of an interest in the land according to the records of the County Register of Deeds.

b. The person(s) in actual open possession of the land.

c. The grantee(s) under *recorded* tax deed for the latest year's taxes.

d. The mortgagee(s) named in all undischarged, *recorded*, mortgages, or any assignee(s) thereof.

e. The holder of record of all undischarged *recorded* liens.

WHO	**DOES WHAT**

f. If the property is improved residential.

NOTE 3: "IMPROVED RESIDENTIAL PARCEL" means a parcel of land which contains a dwelling suitable for occupancy.

NOTE 4: If a person is incompetent, notice is served on his/her trustee or guardian.

NOTE 5: If a person is deceased, notice is served on the executor, trustee or administrator of his/her estate, or on his/her heir(s).

4. Completes Service of Notice substantially in the form set forth in this section and forwards to county sheriff.

NOTE 6: If the property is improved residential, the notice must contain the statement: "This parcel is an improved residential parcel." Failure to include this statement invalidates the notice.

NOTE 7: Service of Notice forms may be obtained at various stationery stores and printing companies.

5. Delivers Service of Notice to sheriff of the county in which person(s) determined in step 3 resides and requests that he/she serve notice on them.

WHO	DOES WHAT

SERVICE OF NOTICE AND SUBSTITUTED NOTICE

Sheriff, Undersheriff, Deputy Sheriff
6. Enters the time and date Service of Notice was delivered to or him/her.

7. Serves notice on person(s) determined in step 3 and returns a copy of the notice to the tax title buyer with the proof of service of notice.

NOTE 8: Service may be made by leaving the notice at that person's place of residence with a member of that person's family of mature age.

NOTE 9: If person(s) to be served resides out of state, sheriff serves notice by certified mail, return receipt requested.

Tax Title Buyer
8. Files notice an sheriff's proof of service with the County Treasurer.

NOTE 10: A fee of $.50 is charged for filing each Proof of Service of Notice or "substituted service."

NOTE 11: The 6 month redemption period commences on the date the notice is filed with the County Treasurer.

IN EVENT THE SHERIFF CANNOT SERVE NOTICE (STEP 7) FOLLOW STEPS 9 and 10.

Sheriff
9. Completes Return of Failure of Service and gives to tax title buyer.

WHO	DOES WHAT
	10. Causes "substituted service of notice" to be published in a newspaper. *NOTE 12: Newspaper must be published and circulated in the county where the land is located. If no such newspaper exists, publication is made in a newspaper published and circulated in an adjoining county. NOTE 13: Publication must be made once each week for 4 consecutive weeks.*
	11. Files Proof of Publication, by affidavit of printer or publisher of the newspaper together with the sheriff's return of Failure of Service, with the County Treasurer. *NOTE 14: If the property is an improved residential property, an extra copy must be filed with the County Treasurer. NOTE 15: Persons with a redeemable interest have six months to redeem following the filing of the proof of service of notice or "substituted service." IMPROVED RESIDENTIAL PROPERTY*
County Treasurer	12. Forwards copy of proof of service of notice to County Department of Social Services for investigation.

WHO   DOES WHAT

SERVICE OF NOTICE ON CORPORATIONS
(STEP #13)

Sheriff, 13. Serves notice on one of the fol-
Undersheriff, lowing where the corporation or
Deputy   maintains its principal registered
Sheriff   office for the transaction of business in this State as indicated by
the articles of incorporation:
a. President
b. Secretary
c. Treasurer
d. Resident agent of corporation, or
e. Person in charge of office.
*NOTE 16: If the president's, sec-
retary's, treasurer's or general
agent's office cannot be located,
follow steps 9 and 10.*
*NOTE 17: This section's provision
applies to corporations whose
term of existence has expired as
well as to those whose term of
existence has not expired.*
*NOTE 18: Notice on foreign corpor-
ations may be served on registered
agent in the county in which its registered office is located, or by certified mail addressed to the corporation at its home office.*

Persons   14. Deposits amount necessary to
with a re-   redeem taxes with the County
deemable Treasurer.
interest   *NOTE 19: Tax Title buyer is required to notify the treasurer of
the personal or substituted service fees.*

WHO	**DOES WHAT**
	NOTE 20: Personal or substituted service fees shall be the same as provided for service of subpoenas, for orders of publication, or for the cost of service by certified mail.
	NOTE 21: The amount necessary to redeem at this point includes:
	a. The amount paid to purchase the lien plus 50%.
	b. $5.00 for each description.
	c. Personal or substituted service fees.
	NOTE 22: The amount necessary to redeem prior to service of notice includes:
	a. The amount paid to purchase the lien plus 50%
	b. $5.00 for each description.
	NOTE 23: The person(s) redeeming the taxes does not acquire any greater interest in the property beyond that which he already has.
County Treasurer	15. Notifies tax title buyer that the amount necessary to redeem the taxes has been deposited.
Tax Title Buyer	16. Executes a release and quitclaim and gives to County Treasurer along with any other papers that pertain to the tax lien involved.
	NOTE 24: Other papers shall include any or all of the following if appropriate:

WHO	DOES WHAT
	a. The tax deed
	b. The purchase certificate
	c. The tax receipts
	d. Any other conveyance relating to tax title or tax interest.
	NOTE 25: The above papers must be surrendered by the tax title buyer before he/she is entitled to receive the redemption money.
County Treasurer	17. Pays the tax title buyer the redemption money.
	18. Forwards items received in step 16 to the person(s) that redeemed the taxes.
Person(s) redeeming taxes	19. Records release and quit-claim at Register of Deeds Office.
	NOTE 26: The Register of Deeds is entitled to the same fees as provided by law for recording deeds of conveyance and other instruments.

PROCEDURE FOR CONVEYANCE
TO TAX TITLE BUYER

County Treasurer	20. After six months redemption expires and at request of tax title buyer, prepares a certified copy of service of notice.
	NOTE 27: The County Treasurer is entitled to the fees as provided by law for preparing the certified copy.
	21. Collects recording fee and transmits service of notice and proof of service of notice and/or "substituted service" to Register of Deeds Office.

WHO	DOES WHAT
	NOTE 28: A $.50 fee is provided for transmitting the service of notice and proof of service of notice, or "substituted service" to the Register of Deeds Office.
Register Deeds	22. Records service of notice and of proof of service of notice, or "substituted service."
	NOTE 29: The Register of Deeds is entitled to the same fees as provided by law for recording deeds of conveyance and other instruments.
	NOTE 30: The recording of the service of notice, proof of service of notice, or "substituted service," and tax deed, is prima facae evidence of the purchaser's title enabling him to seek a writ of assistance from the Circuit Court.
Tax Title Buyer	23. Records tax deed when originally received, or when the service of notice and proof of service of notice, or "substitute service" are recorded.
	NOTE 31: It is recommended that all remaining taxes be paid. Failure of the Person(s) with a redeemable interest (step 3) to redeem the taxes within the six month redemption period bars them from questioning the validity of the tax title or tax deed.

The Local Property Services Division, Department of Treasury, recommends that the preceding procedure be followed. However, the law provides that a person with a redeemable interest may negotiate directly with the tax title buyer.

Phone Numbers to Get You Started

Bay (Bay City)	(517) 895-4286
Genessee (Flint)	(313) 257-3054
Macomb (Warren)	(313) 469-5190
Muskegon (Muskegon)	(616) 724-6261
Oakland (Waterford)	(313) 858-0611

(Ask for the Treasurer's Office)

Mississippi

The Land Tax Sale

In Mississippi, property taxes are due three times per year; one-half (plus all taxes due for bonds) by February 1, one-fourth by May 1 and one-fourth by August 1. For two weeks, a list of delinquent properties will be published in a newspaper, along with the amounts owed. If no newspaper exists in that county, the list will be posted. In either case, the notice will announce a tax lien sale the first Monday in April or the third Monday of September.

§§27-41-1, 27-41-55, 27-41-55, 27-41-57, 27-41-59 (All references are to the Mississippi Code Annotated.)

The sale will take place between 8:30 A.M. and 4:30 P.M. If a large parcel if for sale, the first 40 acres or a smaller subdivision will be sold first. If the buyer does not "immediately pay," he can be sued.

§§27-41-59, 27-41-73

If the sale should be for more than the amount owed, the excess is held in the county treasury. If the property is redeemed, the amount is refunded to the tax lien buyer. If not, then the landowner gets this excess.

§27-41-77

On or before the second Mondays in May and October, a list of sold properties goes to the clerk of the Chancery Court.

REDEMPTION OF THE PROPERTY

The property owner can redeem within two years from the sale. The redemption requires payment of 5% "damages on the amount of taxes for which the land was sold, and interest

§27-45-3

on all such taxes at the rate of one per centum per month, or any fractional part thereof, from the date of such sale, and all taxes and costs that have accrued on the land since the sale . . ."

This interest rate structure allows the buyer the greatest returns on early redemptions. If the redemption occurs in one week, the 6% (5% penalty plus 1% interest) earned would annualize at a (purely theoretical) 312% per year! After earning 17% at the end of the first year, however, the lien earns only 12% per year thereafter.

The two years for redemption is extended for minors and the insane, who can redeem within two years of reaching adulthood or being restored to sanity, respectively. While they can get the property back, they must nevertheless pay the value of any improvements made after two years.

If a mortgage is secured by only part of the land sold, then the mortgage holder is permitted to redeem only that part.

Obtaining a Tax Deed

§27-45-23

At the end of the two-year period, the chancery clerk will, on demand, execute a deed. The tax lien buyer will then get "a perfect title with the immediate right of possession."

§27-45-27

If the sale is invalidated for any reason, the buyer will still get a lien for the 5% penalty plus 12% per year interest.

Phone Numbers to Get You Started

De Soto (Hernando)	(601) 429-1341
Jackson (Pascagoula)	(601) 769-3200
Landerdale (Meridian)	(601) 482-9786
Warren (Vicksburg)	(601) 638-6181

(Ask for the Tax Collector's Office)

New Hampshire

I have found that a tax lien sale has become a rare event in New Hampshire, perhaps because their frugal counties would rather keep the penalties than get the cash. Still, they are authorized by state law, and you might find one.

The Tax Lien Auction

Tax lien auctions may be held both by counties and cities or towns. The bidding is not based upon the percentage return you will get, or on how much you will pay; those are fixed. Rather, "[e]very such sale shall be at auction for the percentage of the common and undivided interest in the whole property that a bidder is willing to offer for the unpaid tax, interest and costs due thereon."

§§80:20-a; 80:24. (All references are to New Hampshire Revised Statutes Annotated.)

The tax collector gives notice of the sale by posting advertisements at two or more public places at least 25 days before the sale. Notice is also to be sent by registered mail to the delinquent taxpayer 30 days before the sale.

§80:21

The sale will take place between the hours of 10:00 A.M. and 6:00 P.M. It can be adjourned for up to three days.

§80:24

The tax collector sends information about the results of the sale to the register of deeds, who will record it.

§80:27

Notification of Mortgage Holder by Buyer

New Hampshire has a unique procedure which can cause a real problem if ignored. Within 45 days of purchase, the *tax lien buyer* must notify mortgage holders, as determined by the county records, of the sale. This notice can be sent in person or by registered mail. Unless this is done, the tax sale is not valid as against the mortgage holder! Nevertheless, even if this notice is not given, the tax lien buyer can sue the taxpayer for the taxes paid.

§§80:28, 80:29

The tax lien buyer may pay subsequent years' taxes. In such a case the mortgage holder must be notified within 30 days of these payments. These subsequent payments also earn interest at the rate of 18%.

§§80:29, 80:37

Redemption of the Property

§§80:30, 80:32, 80:35, 80:37, 80:69

The property may be redeemed by paying the tax collector the amount for which the property was sold, plus 18% interest. Partial redemption payments can be made in multiples of $5.00. Part owners may, if they wish, redeem only their share.

Issuance of Tax Deed

§§80:38, 80:38a

If the property is not redeemed within two years, the tax collector will send notification to the property owner by certified mail. After 30 days, if the property is still not redeemed, the tax collector will issue a deed to the tax certificate buyer.

§80:40

There is a 10 year statute of limitations for contesting the validity of the tax sale and the tax deed.

New Jersey

Tax liens are sold in New Jersey not only by counties, but by every agency which collects taxes. If you are thinking about investing in New Jersey tax lien certificates (called "certificates of purchase" in that state), be sure to review chapter 15 and heed its advice about avoiding environmental liabilities. True, New Jersey calls itself the "Garden State," and true, there is justification for the claim, as much of the state is lovely. At the same time, because of a vigorous yet uncontrolled industrial history, New Jersey has more hazardous waste dump sites per square mile and numerically than any place outside of Eastern Europe.

§§54:5-19, 54:5-21 and 54:5-25 (All section references are to Title 54, New Jersey Codes, Annotated, known as the "Tax Sale Law".)

New Jersey's tax lien certificates pay a healthy 18%, plus a penalty of 2%–6%. Its rules, however, are more complex than those in most states. This summary omits some of the details.

Notice of Tax Lien Sale

Taxes are delinquent on July 1 in the year after they were due. The tax collector makes a list, current as of July 1, of these properties.

A public notice of the tax sale of these properties is given, which contains a description of the lots, the owner's name, and the amount of tax due as of July 1.

The notice of sale must be posted a "five of the most public places in the municipality." (In the Tax Sale Law, any taxing agency is called a "municipality.") In addition, the notice is published in the local newspaper for four weeks before the week of the sale. The notice is also mailed to the property owner.

§§54:5-26, 54:5-27

Conduct of the Sale

The sale is at auction for the amount advertised. "The sale shall be made in fee to such person as will purchase the property, subject to redemption at the lowest rate of interest, but in no case more than 18% per annum." Should anyone be inclined, the bid can be at no interest and even a premium above the taxes. Payment shall be made before the conclusion of the sale. The successful bidder gets a certificate of sale.

§§54:5-31, 54:5-32

§54:5-33

§54:5-46

After two years, no attack, except on the ground of fraud, can be made on the validity of the certificate of sale.

§54:5-52

Recording the Certificate of Sale

Within three months of the date of sale, the buyer should record the certificate of sale in the office of the clerk or registrar of deeds. The certificate is recorded as the equivalent of a mortgage.

§54:5-50-51

Unless this recording is made, the property owner can wipe out this certificate by selling the property to a "bona fide purchaser" (that is, one without notice of your lien), or leasing or mortgaging the property to persons without notice of the lien.

Redemption by Property Owner

The property owner can simply pay the taxes before the sale. If the sale goes forward, the property owner can redeem within 10 days of the sale by paying the amount you paid at the sale plus interest. After ten days, the property owner who wants to redeem must also pay (if you give an affidavit) sub-

§§54:5-29, 54:5-58-54:5-62

sequent municipal liens which you may have paid, plus a penalty of 2% if the cost to redeem is over $200, 4% if it is over $5,000 and 6% if the cost to redeem is over $10,000.

§54:5-54

This redemption can be made, not only by the property owner, but also by a "mortgagee, occupant or other person having an interest in the land sold for municipal liens."

The right to redeem extends for "2 years from the date of sale when the purchaser is other than the municipality, or at any time thereafter until the right to redeem is cut off."

§§54:5-55,
54:5-57

If a redemption occurs, a certificate of redemption is issued, which may be recorded. Your certificate of sale is canceled. You will be notified and paid the redemption monies upon your "surrender" of the certificate of sale.

Foreclosing on the Lien

§§54:5-77,
54:5-114.4

After the right to redeem expires, you will foreclose. After 20 years, further action is barred. Written notice is given to the property owner of his right to redeem. The notice will state that if no redemption occurs within certain time limits, the right to redeem will be barred.

§54:5-77

These time limits are two years after the date of the sale, provided that notice is made within 18 months of the date of the sale; or six months from the date of the notice, if the notice is given after 18 months of the sale.

The property owner must be served personally if he resides within the municipality. Service can be personal or by mail if the owner does not reside there. If the location of the owner is unknown, then service will be by posting the notice on the premises or in the office of the tax collector and "three other conspicuous places." If service is not made personally, then the notice must also be published once in the newspaper.

§54:5-78

If the property owner still does not redeem the property within the time given in the notice, the right to redeem is barred.

§54:5-79

On the other hand, if you do not foreclose within 20 years of the purchase, you are barred from foreclosing, unless you paid all property taxes each year.

§54:5-80

Once the right to redeem is barred, you attach to your certificate of sale: (1) your notice to the property owner, (2) affidavits of service and publication of the notice, (3) your affidavit that the property was not redeemed, (4) an official certificate (which will cost you $1.00) that the property was not redeemed and (5) the results of an official search showing that all subsequent certificates have been paid. You take this to the county clerk or register "where they shall be recorded as a deed of conveyance."

After two years, and absent fraud, there can be no attack on the service of your notice or other irregularities, except by minors or incompetents.

§54:5-81

If you want your title to be safe from minors and incompetents too, you need to foreclose in the superior court. To do this, you must give 30 days notice of the intent to file a complaint and the amount due, or else you will not receive your filing fee and counsel fees if you go ahead and sue. After you get your judgment of foreclosure and after three months, except on the grounds of lack of jurisdiction or fraud there can be no application to reopen the judgment.

§§54:5-84,
54:5-97.1,
54:5-104.64(b),
54:5-104.76

Unsold Liens

Liens which are not sold at the auction can be sold by the municipality at a private sale or at another auction for not less than the amount of the liens or, if the liens are for more than the assessed value, then for the assessed value. By resolution, the municipality can sell at a lower price.

§54:5-113

A statute enacted in December 1993 allows one or more municipalities to package and sell tax lien certificates and sell them on terms. The first sale as a $44 million page sold by Jersey City to CS First Boston Corporation.

If you do buy from the municipality, pay careful attention to the rules, because special time limits then apply to redemption and foreclosure, and if you miss your limit and have not gotten an extension of time to foreclose from the municipality, you will lose what you paid for the lien!

§§54:5-113–54:
5-114.6

Defective Liens

§54:5-42

If the tax sale is voided, a lien for what you paid nevertheless continues in effect.

§54:5-43

Even if the sale was defective, the sale cannot be set aside unless the tax is paid, along with interest and charges.

§§54:5-104.100

When you buy at a defective tax sale and intend to occupy the property, special rules apply.

New Jersey is not as generous as some states, which will have the taxing agency pay you a certain rate of interest itself if the sale is void because of some fault of that agency.

Phone Numbers to Get You Started

Bridgetown	(609) 455-3230
Fleminton	(908) 782-8840
Garfield	(201) 340-2103
Newton	(201) 383-3524
Paterson	(201) 881-3450

(Ask for the Tax Collector's Office)

North Dakota

Burleigh County, North Dakota, publishes a good summary of that state's tax lien certificate program. Because that summary leaves out some important facts, I will add them at the end.

North Dakota Century Code Chapters 57-24 to 57-27

SALE OF TAX CERTIFICATES

Every 2nd Tuesday in December a sale of the current year's delinquent taxes is held. If no one purchases these certificates they are automatically purchased by the County.

Notice of the sale is given by publication in the official paper of the county once each week for

---

two consecutive weeks, and by posting in at least four public places.

This sale is held in the office of the county auditor, with the minimum price equaling the amount of delinquent taxes. Those persons paying the delinquent taxes receive a tax sale certificate. The owner of a tax sale certificate may pay the taxes upon the property described in such certificate for any subsequent year at any time that they become delinquent. Upon payment of any such taxes, with accrued penalties and costs thereon, that person is entitled to a "subsequent tax sale certificate." Only the holder of the original tax sale certificate can purchase subsequent sale certificates.

Any person or corporation or any heir or creditor of an owner who dies having an interest in the property sold at a tax certificate sale may redeem the real estate sold. Redemption price shall be the amount paid at the tax sale plus interest at a rate of 12% annually for the original and 9% for the subsequent tax sale certificates.

Any person holding a tax sale certificate, at any time after the expiration of three years and before ten years from the date of the tax sale to which such tax certificate relates, may present such certificate to the county auditor, who shall then prepare a notice to the person in whose name the lands described are assessed and all mortgagees etc., stating when such redemption expires. The notice of expiration shall be delivered to the Sheriff who shall serve it or cause it to be served personally upon the owner, if known to be a resident of the state, but if known not to be a resident of the state the notice shall be served by registered or certified mail and by publication once each week for three consecutive weeks in the official newspaper of the county. The notice shall also

be served personally upon any person actually residing on the property. Duplicate copies shall be
mailed to any mortgagee etc., if requested in writing.

The period of expiration shall expire ninety
(90) days after the completion of the service of the
notice of expiration.

If no redemption is made within this ninety (90)
days, upon surrender of the tax sale certificate to
the county auditor and upon payment of all other
delinquent taxes, a tax deed shall be issued.

SYNOPSIS OF TAX CERTIFICATE SALE

1) Current year's tax certificates available
after 2nd Tuesday in December.

2) Purchaser receives tax sale certificate.

3) Upon redemption purchaser receives
amount paid plus interest (12% annually for
original).

4) Only holder of original certificate can purchase subsequent certificates (9% interest
for subsequent).

5) After holding original for three (3) years
and before ten (10) years certificate holder
can start action.

6) Property owner has ninety day redemption rights after action started.

7) If no redemption within ninety days holder
of certificate entitled to a Tax Deed.

§57-24-29(4)   At the North Dakota auction, the winning bidder is the
one who will accept the lowest rate of interest.

§57-24-21   Tax sale certificates are, as in other states, assignable. The
assigned certificate may be (and certainly should be) presented to the county auditor.

§57-27-07   If no sale is made at the auction, the county auditor can

sell the unbought certificates. However, these certificate will only pay 6% per year!

§57-26-04

One cannot be absolutely certain that no redemption will occur after the redemption period has expired, because mentally ill persons, minors and prisoners of war can redeem within three years after their disability ends.

Phone Numbers to Get You Started

Burleigh (Bismark)	(701) 222-6718
Cass (Fargo)	(701) 241-5600
Ward (Minot)	(701) 857-6417
Statsman (Jamestown)	(701) 252-9035

(Ask for the County Auditor's Office)

Wyoming

Wyoming is another state where you do not bid the amount of interest you will get, nor even the amount of cash you will pay, but rather the extent of the interest in the property you will accept. What you receive is a Certificate of Purchase *of the property*. This is just a fiction though, because the owner has four years to redeem, after which you may apply for a Tax Deed.

When Taxes Are Delinquent

One-half of the property tax is due in Wyoming on November 1, and the other half is due on May 10. The tax is delinquent as of May 11. A list of delinquent taxes is prepared by May 21.

§§39-3-101, 39-3-102 (All section references are to the Wyoming Statutes.)

Rate of Interest

Delinquent taxes bear a rate of interest of 18% per year.

§39-3-102

Conduct of the Auction

§39-3-103

The auction of Certificates of Purchase is advertised once each week for three weeks in a legal newspaper. The first publication must be four weeks before the sale and conclude before the first week in September.

§39-3-105

The auction is held at the county courthouse between 9:00 A.M. and 5:00 P.M., except on Sundays.

The Certificate of Purchase is sold to "[a]ny person who offers to pay the amount of taxes, interest, penalties and costs including charges . . . for the smallest portion of the real property . . ."

The successful bidder must "immediately" pay the county treasurer.

§39-3-105

The buyer will get a Certificate of Purchase which is entered by number in the county rolls.

Unsold Certificates

§39-3-107

Any certificates that are not sold go the county treasurer. The county may resell those certificates "at public or private sale at any time."

Assignment of Certificates

§39-3-105

You may assign you Certificates of Purchase to another person by endorsing them.

Redemption by Property Owner

§39-3-108

If the property is "sold" (that is, if a Certificate of Purchase is issued) the property owner may redeem the property within four years from the date of sale. If the property owner does redeem, he gets a Certificate of Redemption. The county treasurer will then notify you of the redemption.

Obtaining a "Tax Deed"

§39-3-108

At least four years, but not more than six years, after you get your Certificate of Purchase, you may apply to the county treasurer for a Tax Deed.

To do this, at least three months beforehand, you must have completed service of notice on each person in possession of the property and each person in whose name the property was taxed or assessed, as well as the mortgage holders. The service on the owners can be by publication if they cannot be served personally.

Service by publication requires that the notice be published once per week for three weeks, the first publication occurring not more than five months before the application for the tax deed. You must also send a notice by certified or registered mail to the owners of record and the mortgage holders.

The notice you give must contain the following information:

(a) When you "purchased" the property (i.e., when you got your Certificate of Purchase).
(b) In whose name the property was taxed.
(c) The legal description of the property.
(d) The year the property was taxed or assessed.
(e) When the time of redemption will expire.
(f) When an application for a Tax Deed will be made.
(g) The amount of any special assessment for local or public improvements.

After the notification process is complete and you have waited three months, you can return the Certificate of Purchase, pay the required fees, and prove your compliance with the notice provisions. Proof of service by publication requires the sworn statement of the newspaper's publisher, manager, or editor.

Once you have done all this, you will receive a Tax Deed. *§39-3-106* As the holder of a Tax Deed, you are entitled to possession of the property.

If the Tax Deed Is Attacked

Occasionally, a Certificate of Purchase or a Tax Deed is issued in error. For example, the property owner may have paid the tax, and the county forgot to record it.

If the sale is void because of a mistake by the County *§39-3-201* Treasurer, the county will pay you what you would have received upon a redemption.

§39-3-202

If the sale is void for some other reason, you are given a lien carrying 8% interest. This lien is for your payments of taxes, costs, penalties, interest, and the value of improvements to the property which you may have made. This lien is superior to all other liens, except those created by other tax sales or the payment of taxes by another person. You can foreclose on this lien and have the property sold. At the sale, you can bid in the amount of your lien.

Note: "The Tax Sale Purchaser's Lien," 4 Wyo. L. J. 275, 277 (1950)

The lien can be foreclosed between four and ten years after the original purchase. If no taxes were ever due however, you cannot foreclose, but must look to the county to pay for its mistake.

Phone Numbers to Get You Started

Laramie (Cheyenne)	(307) 638-4225
Natronia (Casper)	(307) 235-9470
Sweetwater (Green River)	(307) 875-5832

(Ask for the Treasurer's Office)

APPENDIX III
Environmental Forms for Commercial and Industrial Properties

As I discussed in chapter 14, one of the advantages of specializing your investments in residential properties is that they require far less investigation.

Nevertheless, because commercial and industrial properties may present very attractive opportunities, I have included two forms to get you started in checking out these properties.

The first of these forms is a "Pre-Audit Environmental Questionnaire," which poses some initial questions about the property, and may reveal disqualifying problems immediately. The second form is a "Phase 1 Consultant Contract," which you can use to engage environmental professionals to assist you.

Should you be drawn to investments in commercial and industrial properties, you should consider obtaining my book *Environmental Liabilities and Real Property Transactions* (John Wiley & Sons), which contains several more useful forms, along with a complete treatment of environmental issues, updated twice each year. You may contact me c/o the publisher of this book or call John Wiley & Sons directly.

Form 1:
Pre-Audit Environmental Questionnaire

1. *Facility address:* _____

_____

2. *Contact at facility:* Name: _____

Phone: _____

3. *Property owner:* _____

4. *Zoning*: _____

5. *Property size:* _____

6. *Tenants:*	Company name	Building number

7. *Buildings:*	Building number	Uses	Square feet	**Age**

8. *Previous uses of site:* _____

_____

_____

_____

_____

_____

_____

9. *Are any underground tanks currently located at the facility?*

Yes _____ No _____

10. *If the answer to #9 is "Yes" then for each tank list:*

Contents   Age   Size   Type of Construction   Date last tested

_____

_____

_____

11. *Hazardous materials present on property:*

_____

_____

_____

_____

12. *Is electrical equipment (e.g., transformers, light ballasts) on the property which may contain PCBs?*

Yes _____ No _____

13. *If the answer to #12 is "Yes," is any of this equipment leaking?*

Yes _____ No _____

14. *Do any of the buildings on the site contain asbestos?*

Yes _____ No _____

15. *If the answer to #14 is "Yes," is the asbestos in apparently good condition?*

Yes _____ No _____

16. *List the types of businesses bordering the property:*

Business   Location

_____

_____

_____

_____

_____

_____

17. *Have any of these neighboring properties had a release of hazardous substances or any other environmental problems?*

Yes _____ No _____

18. *If the answer to #17 is "Yes," please describe (use separate sheet if necessary):*

_____

_____

_____

_____

_____

19. *Is any disposal site for garbage or other wastes located on or within 2,000 feet of the property?*

Yes _____ No _____

20. *If the answer to #19 is "Yes," please indicate the location and nature of the materials at the site:*

_____

_____

_____

_____

_____

_____

21. *List each location on the property where hazardous materials have been at any time stored, treated, disposed of or released:*

Location   Nature of activity or release

_____

_____

_____

_____

_____

_____

22. *Has any notice been issued by a government agency concerning an investigation of possible contamination of the property or the violation of any environmental laws?*

Yes _____ No _____

23. *If the answer to #22 is "Yes," explain below the date and nature of each such notice:*

_____

_____

_____

_____

_____

24. *Please attach to this questionnaire:*

a. Construction plans and specifications, if available;

b. A site layout, if available;

c. Any environmental study performed on the property;

d. Any claims or notices concerning environmental conditions on or about the property.

Form 2
"Phase 1" Consultant Contract

Whereas _____ [*name of investor*] ("Investor") requires an expert consultant in connection with its investigation of environmental conditions at _____ [*address of property*] (the "Property");

Whereas _____ [*name of consultant*] ("Consultant") has the required expertise and desires to assist Investor in this investigation:

Therefore, Investor and Consultant agree as follows:

Consultant will perform a "Phase 1" preliminary environmental assessment on the Property which is designed to provide information concerning the possible presence of environmental conditions on the Property which may require investigation of remediation under, or which may violate, federal, state or local statutes, regulations or policies, including the presence of chemical contamination on or under the Property. This assessment will include:

(1) a walk-through inspection of the Property;

(2) examination of historic aerial photographs and other information revealing past uses of and the potential presence of hazardous materials on the Property;

(3) an examination of the records of relevant federal, state or local agencies to determine whether the Property, of locations neighboring the Property, have been placed on a list of contaminated properties, including but not limited to the CERCLIS list, the National Priorities List, and any list of locations with leaking underground storage tanks;

(4) an examination of pertinent government permitting files to determine whether a permit for an underground storage tank, a hazardous waste generator's number, or any other permit for the treatment, storage or disposal of hazardous materials has ever been issued with respect to the Property;

(5) interviews with persons knowledgeable concerning the historic uses of the Property.

Consultant will provide a report to Investor concerning its findings on the above matters within _____ days from the date of this contract.

Consultant shall be paid for its services under this contract at its usual and customary rates, which amount shall not exceed $ _____.

Consultant will keep the results of its investigations, including its report, confidential and shall not disclose such results or report to any person or entity, including any governmental entity, except as required by law.

Consultant shall not assign this contract to any person or entity without the express consent of Investor.

Investor may cancel this contract at any time, by delivery of written notice to Consultant, or if the notice is oral, upon actual receipt of such notice. Upon such cancellation, Consultant shall be entitled to fees earned up to the time of delivery or receipt of such notice.

Consultant shall perform its services as an independent contractor, and not as an employee of Investor. Consultant shall obtain and maintain worker's compensation insurance in the amount required by the state wherein the Property is located, and general liability and automobile liability insurance in the amount of $1,000,000 per occurrence, which policy shall name Investor as an additional insured.

No waiver by Investor or Consultant of any term of this contract shall be a waiver of any future or other default of any term of this contract. If any portion of this contract is determined to be invalid, the remainder of this contract shall not be affected, and shall be enforced to the fullest extent allowed by law.

This contract contains the entire understanding of the parties, and all other agreements or contracts, written or oral, are superseded by this contract. No modification of this contract shall be made, except by a writing executed by all parties to this contract.

Date: _____ _____
                                                    [signature of Investor]

                                      _____
                                                    [signature of Consultant]

APPENDIX IV
Further Information

The following firm provides a brokerage service for those wanting to sell their tax lien certificates, and those wanting to buy them on the secondary market. It specializes in Colorado and Florida:

American Tax Lien Exchange, Inc.
P.O. Box 88205
Colorado Springs, Colorado 80908-8205
(719) 495-9190

New Jersey's rich variety of tax lien activities is covered in a newsletter, "Tax Lien Investor," which provides current coverage of the dates of tax lien sales in that state and other useful information. Subscriptions are currently $65.00 per year plus $3.90 tax.

Tax Lien Investors Association of New Jersey
12-B The Ellipse Building #240
4201 Church Road
Mount Laurel, NJ 08054
(609) 234-2080

Those focusing on tax lien certificates in Arizona and Iowa will be interested in How to Invest in Arizona Tax Liens and How to Invest in Iowa Tax Liens, by John N. Beck. Copies are available for $99.50 + $5.00 shipping and California sales tax from:

MGC Capital Group
2845 Chippewa Ave.
Simi Valley, CA 93063
(805) 526-2443

About the Author

Joel S. Moskowitz has been practicing law for 22 years. At present, he is a partner at Gibson, Dunn & Crutcher, an environmental law firm and one of the largest firms in the United States.

Between 1970 and 1983, Joel Moskowitz was a deputy attorney general for the state of California. For two years, he served California's governor as chief of the toxic substances control programs.

Mr. Moskowitz is the author of numerous publications on law and real estate, including *Environmental Liability and Real Property Transactions* (John Wiley & Sons).